Butterflies, Bubbles, and Bird Nests

Finding God's Loving Kindness
in the Ordinary:
77 Devotions with Scripture and Prayer

Cynthia Holloway

ISBN 979-8-88943-730-7 (paperback)
ISBN 979-8-89130-189-4 (hardcover)
ISBN 979-8-88943-732-1 (digital)

Christian Faith Publishing
832 Park Avenue
Meadville, PA 16335
www.christianfaithpublishing.com

Printed in the United States of America

Dedication

Where would I be without my heavenly Father? He is the
reason for my being. Even when I have lost my way at times,
God has always been there extending His lovingkindness
in various ways. I am truly humbled and grateful for
His fatherly love, which extends into all of eternity.

I deeply cherish the love and support of my family, my
friends, and those precious and near to my heart.

Thank you, God, for the stories. May I never take them for granted.

Love to my hubby, my sibbies, and my Christian heroes!

Contents

Author's Note

Dear reader,

Thank you for taking the time to read and for letting God speak to you through my stories given by God. As was in my first book, *Fingerprints of God: 62 Day Devotional to Finding God in Ordinary Circumstances*, this book, *Butterflies, Bubbles, and Bird Nests: Finding God's Lovingkindness in the Ordinary,* is a result of my own journaling during ordinary live events and times of joy and sorrow. Never in my wildest dreams did I imagine authoring a devotional book, let alone write anything at all. It was *only God* who allowed this to happen in my life as He gently spoke and encouraged me in my spirit and provided a way.

I believe that for every believer, God is in control of our lives as long as we are striving to seek His will and way. Things will happen, life will not be easy at times, but if we are hand in hand with *the only God* of both earth and heaven, then we can be assured He will give us all we need when we need it. His lovingkindness and extended grace are unending!

As you read, let the stories sink into your heart. You may relate to some more than others, but the important thing is that you grasp the magnificence of God and the ways He desires to work in your life. Trust that He is yearning to show you love and affection, and His hands are always open to receiving you right where you are! He will show up in ordinary circumstances and leaves His fingerprints along the journey. Always be watchful for Him to amaze you in all areas of your life. I wish multiple blessings to you as you read!

Thy lovingkindness, O Lord, extends to the heavens, Thy faithfulness reaches to the skies. (Psalm 36:5 NAS)

With heartfelt love and appreciation,
Cynthia

Selfish Agendas

(God and Jesus are used interchangeably
throughout this devotion.)

Do you ever think about how selfish and busy your daily agenda might be that there is no room for Jesus? Life is busy, that is for sure. But I am wondering how different our day might be or go if we really allowed Jesus to have liberty regarding our daily to do list. What if He doesn't want us *doing* anything? What if He just wants us to be with Him? Would that be enough for you and make your day feel complete? This doesn't mean we are to give up our jobs or source of income, family, worship etc. Jesus can be found in all those places. I am speaking about filling our lives with needless things of doing.

Our spirits are crying out, I believe, for peace, assurance, joy, and contentment—all the things that God wants to give us. How can we have those things if we aren't seeking them from the one who is the source of all those things? What if we were to give Him more priority over our ofttimes selfish daily agendas? Wonder what wonderful things He might reveal to us all because we chose to spend time with Him? The presence of God is always with us, but there is no way we can really get to know Him unless we are spending quality time with Him. Attending church and worship accounts for some, but it isn't enough. We have to be growing, learning, seeking, reading, and searching for Him in all things.

God wants to add fresh stories to our lives. He wants us to experience Him in amazing ways. If we have a full daily agenda, where is there room for God? Today, I am challenging you to begin spending some quality time with God every single day. He is only a breath away. Call out to Him in the quiet of your heart. Enjoy what He says to you in your spirit. Do not be afraid to speak your dreams, your concerns, and your desires.

This sacred time is not about other people; this time is just for you and Jesus. It is to be intimate. You might be surprised of all the exciting ways He will bless you and reward you in your life and spirit all because you chose to come to Him. Seek out places where you can go to meet Him. Take a walk, sit quietly in the sun, rest in the shade, have a nice cup of coffee as you read a devotion, or seek the sanctity of your closet if you so choose. Just be with Him, the giver of everything. May your agenda allow room for Jesus each and every day.

Prayer: Oh, Lord, forgive me when I am so quick to fill up my agenda and not leave any room for you. My time with you is precious. Help me this day to make it a priority in my life. Amen.

Reflective scripture: "Many are the plans in a person's heart, but it is the Lord's purpose that prevails" (Proverbs 19:21 NIV).

In the Driver's Seat

Off in the car we go! On our way to the groomer's for my dog's wash and style. In the seat, he bounces full of anticipation of where we might be going. He does not tend to figure out the destination until we have rounded a certain corner. Until then, he anxiously waits in his special seat upfront with me, his dog mom.

I turn the dial to the soft music channel and settle in for the forty-minute drive. I notice I am always aware of my dog's comfort level in the car. At times, he is curiously sitting upright in his seat, looking around and probably thinking in his doggy mind how he would like to chase that bird he now sees flying overhead. Other times throughout the trip, he settles down and is happy to trust me with the driving and where we might be going.

It made me think about how we need to trust Jesus with our destinations in life—I mean, really trust Him! We, in our limited human minds, tend to become anxious and pace about when we are not in the driver's seat. We especially do not like it when we can't see where we are going. It is hard sometimes to trust that the destination God is leading us to will be worth the journey and will have its rewards in the end. God will make us as comfortable as possible, but we too have to do all we can in preparation for the adventure. The destination might not always be a pleasant one, for life is full of times of uncertainty, but if we can settle down a bit, relax, and stay with God, then the destination is sure to hold many special surprises in store.

Sometimes it is very hard to relax and trust that God is with us, but know that He really is. God will rule out in the end if we are just patient enough and can relax even when we are not the one driving.

Begin today to start letting go a bit. Curl up and imagine yourself just letting God do the driving in your life. Stay filled up by reading His Word, praying, journaling, or talking with a Christian friend about what God reveals to you. Fellowship with other believers and share your stories. May you take comfort in knowing that God is quite capable of getting you to the right destination on time!

Prayer: Dear God, help me let go in areas of my life that cause me to be anxious and upset. May I learn how to relax in You, trusting that all will be well despite any bumps in the road.

Reflective scripture: "For I know the plans I have for you" declares the Lord, "plans to prosper you and not to harm you, plans to give you hope and a future" (Jeremiah 29:11 NIV).

Mission Accomplished

It is nearing sunset, and the glow of the sky is calling me to take a ride in my golf cart through the peaceful scenery of my neighborhood. My dog is curled up beside me as I back us out of the garage and head toward the dog park. We passed various other people riding bikes, walking their dogs, and riding golf carts. I smile and wave at others as the cool breeze blows my dog's ears flip-flap against his face.

Nearing the dog park, my buddy is anxious to begin his adventure, and I let him wander around, sniffing various things that are curious to dogs. I gaze up at the sky and capture a beautiful picture of the sunset through the trees. What a perfect ending to a relaxing day! I feel so blessed sometimes to be able to see the magnificent things of God, don't you?

As we headed toward home, my thoughts began to wander and ponder about the various mission assignments in life we are all given. I felt very humbled at that moment, knowing that God could have me anywhere, doing who knows what instead of driving myself around on my golf cart. I know it is all relative. Some may not think riding around at sunset on a golf cart is anything special, but it was a blessing to me this night to see the simple things of God.

As believers, we are all given mission assignments throughout our lives. Our mission field in life will allow each of us to experience different things. But whatever your assignment, it is important to recognize God at work in *it*, whatever *it* might be. Your *it* will be different from mine, but everything God has assigned us to do is important.

You will, of course, encounter events, people, and experiences that I never will. But all work and encounters are important for God. Encounters are assignments from God, I believe. It takes all of us working as agents for God to get His message of love out to other people. I know that even while riding a golf cart, I can experience God. I know that the people I smiled at earlier or spoke to could have been my assignment for this evening, or perhaps God just wanted me to experience something wonderful. He does that, too, for us.

What were other people doing at this time of night? Why was I given this relaxing opportunity when there are others who are hurting in this world right now? I do not know the answers to these questions, but I do know that our life assignments are serious business. Trust that God has various assignments for you, and He needs you to help accomplish His mission in life. God needs you, your skills, your gifts, and your encouragement to help spread His message. He will reward you in the end as He says, "Mission accomplished."

Prayer: Dear God, open my heart to be receptive to the assignment You have for me this day. Use me to be effective in the lives of others.

Reflective scripture: "His lord said unto him, Well done, thou good and faithful servant: thou hast been faithful over a few things, I will make thee ruler over many things: enter thou into the joy of thy lord" (Matthew 25:21 KJV).

Is It Safe?

It's 3:45 a.m., and my brain is suddenly awake. Yep, just like that, awake!

As I rolled over after looking at the clock, my first thought was, *Is it safe?* "Is what safe?" I ask myself. I knew I was to write a devotion with that title, which was strange because I do not usually get those ideas in the middle of the night. So I got up and wrote my thoughts down, knowing I would have to reflect on this after perhaps feeling more rested and having coffee.

Later in the day, I remembered once having traveled to West Virginia to see my absolute best of friends. She lived at the foothills of a beautiful mountain, and there was a ridiculously small bridge that crossed over a rapidly running body of water… Okay, it was a creek, but I was afraid to cross the bridge in my car. The bridge seemed ill prepared to manage the weight of my car, and I was not sure any more about crossing even after my friend shouted that it was safe because her husband had built it! I trusted my friend and the handiwork of her husband, so I proceeded to cross the bridge with hesitation and caution.

God sometimes asks us to cross bridges that might feel unsafe at time. You see, problems in life can cause us to feel at times a bit creaky, a little wobbly, and unsure about ourselves. We wonder if we have what it takes to sustain and hold up. But if we could see God as our bridge holding us up under pressure and sustaining us in life, then we can proceed with caution and trust that we are safe. God is strong enough to hold the troubles that weigh us down in life. God is the bridge holding us ever steadfast when we are fearful.

Just as my friend was beckoning me to "come and cross over, it's safe," know that God has you in the palm of His hand, and He is calling you to be in fellowship with Him. He will carry you through the rough waters just as He walks with you through the calm. He wants to journey with you and to be ever present in your life. Yes, you are safe with Him, and may you know it to be true today!

Prayer: God, I want You to journey with me throughout the remainder of my life. Thank You for the times when You were my bridge, leading me to safety and peace.

Reflective scripture: "I will lift up my eyes to the mountains-where does my help come from? My help comes from the Lord, the Maker of heaven and earth. He will not let your foot slip-he who watches over you will not slumber" (Psalm 121:1–3 NIV).

God Has You Where You Need to Be

Sometimes in life, we can become frustrated because things in our life are not moving along as we feel they should. We should not react to life events or frustrations based on our feelings. Feelings are a human part of our design, but we cannot always trust them. We need to trust God, not our feelings.

Right now, I am a bit frustrated as to how my first book is not progressing as it pertains to the final proof and print. It is taking longer than anticipated. I can do all I can to make sure people on the other end are held accountable, but the rest is in God's hands. The same holds true for when we question if we are where we need to be in life. If we are a follower of Christ, we can be sure that God has us right where He wants us at any given time. We can worry and fret, but this will only serve to cause us emotional distress as well as possible physical distress.

Tending to look further down the road other than where God currently has us can also cause unnecessary worry. When we take our eyes off God, we become bombarded in our thoughts of the what-ifs in life. *What if this happens or that happens?* could easily become our internal dialogue. Instead, of racing ahead of God, try to pace yourself, slow down in the moment, and ask God to reveal to you what He would have you do. Trust that He is already ahead of you, preparing the way that you should step. It is important to not always be caught up in the doing of life. Sometimes, all we should strive to do is relax and know that God has us right where He wants us. Let that be enough for today.

Prayer: Dear God, please forgive my tendencies to rush ahead of You. Forgive me for attempting to figure things out on my own instead of awaiting Your direction. May peace and reassurance be mine this day according to Your will. Amen.

Reflective scripture: "Come to me, all who are weary and burdened, and I will give you rest" (Matthew 11:28 NIV).

Lotions, Potions, and a Little Pink Bible

Growing older, aw, we all get to do it if we are fortunate enough. Some will never get the privilege, and it really is a privilege. That is not to say that looking into a mirror and seeing new wrinkles appear here and there and seeing the skin not looking as taut as it once was is not hard for some. It is, me included. I sometimes search for that magical potion or lotion that will be effective, but there comes a point where my vain self must accept the inevitable truth of growing older.

If we are fortunate, we have had the blessing of watching loved ones or people we admire grow older and gracefully accept their wrinkles and aging of various forms. I watched my mother battle cancer with grace and bravery, and the only comment I ever heard her make regarding her age was that she would like to get her eyes lifted and her teeth fixed. She did get her teeth fixed, and that helped her to feel better about herself.

I watched too as she read her Bible and grew older in her faith and contemplated her death and afterlife. That said more to me than anything as I watched her end her day by opening her small pink Bible to the psalms. She would read a passage each night before she was tucked into bed by either my sister or myself after becoming too sick to be by herself. She enjoyed lotion on her face and body, but what really made her face glow was the glow of knowing Christ. She knew how to put on Jesus!

Putting on Jesus every day can be challenging in this life. But if we love Him, we will strive to be more like Him. No one said it would be easy, but we must try! May you find comfort in knowing that the God who created you loves you just as you are, wrinkles and all. This earthly life is only preparing us for the heavenly life where we are promised a new body. Isn't that exciting? We will not need lotions and potions, for we will glow in the reflection of Christ.

Until then, read the Bible, memorize scripture, sing, dance in the Lord, and glow in the glory of having God as your Father. You might just want to buy yourself a little pink Bible too.

Prayer: May the glow of You, God, outshine any wrinkles that I might have. May others see Jesus in me this day. Help me when life becomes demanding to remember that You care about every aspect of my life and that scripture and prayer will help me to move forward. Amen.

Reflective scripture: "Even to your old age and gray hairs I am he, I am he who will sustain you. I have made you and I will carry you; I will sustain you and I will rescue you" (Isaiah 46:4 NIV).

Reflecting Jesus

I watched patiently as she interacted with the customer ahead of me. As the resister spat out the receipt, the employee explained how many gas points the customer had accumulated and thanked her for shopping. The employee had chatted with the customer throughout the assorted items that she rang up, slung down the conveyer belt, and bagged. She was oblivious to the line that had formed as other anxious shoppers were awaiting their turn.

My turn. I offered to bag my own groceries, and the cashier lady seemed appreciative. I noticed how fast she could sling my various purchases as they spun around on the conveyer belt due to my lack of keeping up. I could tell the employee enjoyed having only one task to focus on—ringing me up! I watched too as she smiled and seemed to be enjoying her job. I instantly concluded that she was a nice lady. Sometimes you can just tell that about a person, can't you?

As the lady exchanged pleasantries with my husband, I quietly reflected on how I had observed her earlier exchange with the person ahead of me in line, how she took her time, looked her in the eye, and shared how much money she had saved by shopping there. This lady was proud of her job! I liked her genuine smile, and her joyful spirit showed through her eyes as she thanked me for helping to bag.

Sometimes you just know when Christ is alive in someone else's life. I know in my heart that this woman knew Jesus. It was her actions, for she said little. In my spirit, I felt challenged to do better. How about you? Where are you a reflection of Jesus?

Prayer: Lord, help me to reflect Your love. Help me to smile even when life get mundane and routine. May someone be positively influenced by my actions today. Amen.

Reflective scripture: "Examine yourselves to see whether you are in the faith; test yourselves. Do you not realize that Christ Jesus is in you—unless, of course, you fail the test?" (2 Corinthians 13:5 NIV).

Patience and Prayers

Driving down the highway, I was just one of hundreds of people headed to the beach. I am keeping up with the steady flow of traffic, listening to relaxing music, and catching up on my plans for the weekend. I watch as several drivers get impatient and pass a driver who seems to be stuck at a slower mph than the rest of us. One after the other passes this driver, who has favored the left lane for the last two or three miles.

I move over to the right side, staying a distance behind the slower left lane driver. I watch as a huge garbage truck flashes his lights on the tail bumper of the car, trying to intimidate the driver to move over. The person does not bother to move, maintains slow speed, and ignores or does not see the garbage truck's approach from behind. I now have the car in my rearview mirror, and farther ahead, I see what appears to be a bad accident on the left side of the highway. I look behind me and see that the slower car is now turning to cross over the highway to the accident. No doubt, that person had a family member or friend in the accident. That would explain why the driver insisted on remaining in the left lane. They likely were not familiar with the turn and did not want to miss it.

We never know, of course, what another person is going through. I have no real proof that the slowed car was going to that accident, but it appeared so, and God spoke to my spirit to pray. Pray at once for the people involved in the accident and the people helping. God gives us many opportunities to pray for others on daily basis. He also speaks to us in numerous ways to slow down and be anxious for nothing. God has us all on different *speeds*, and when we rush about, oblivious to His warning signs of needing to slow down, we get into trouble.

Let God's patience rule your life. He knows where you need to be and when you need to arrive. Take time to pray for someone today that you might see along the way. Your prayer from a distance could give them the comfort they need. After all, where would we be if not for the prayers of others?

Prayer: Thank You, God, for the people who have slowed down long enough to pray for me over my lifetime. May I, too, be aware of the importance of patience, slowing down, and praying for others. Amen.

Reflective scripture: "Confess your trespasses to one another, and pray for one another, that you may be healed. The effective, fervent prayer of a righteous man avails much" (James 5:16 NKJV).

The Calling

The screen door is open on this rainy August day. Such a quiet, peace-filled morning, until a bird starts calling out, and then another answers the call with his or her own beautiful voice. The random banter lasts for a few minutes, a beautiful sound mixed with the falling rain. The sounds have now become enhanced by the deer I see walking through the nearby field, headed to my backyard, no doubt to partake of the various flowers and foliage.

Nature—thank You, God, for it! It calls out to our hearts and is just like Christ speaking to us individually when we pause and take the time to listen and observe. Do not take for granted the sights and sounds of God's creations. Some people will never get this privilege.

God's Word tells us He created life for our enjoyment. Take the time today to read the entire story of creation in Genesis 1:1–31 and be amazed. Are you pausing long enough in this hurried world to really enjoy the gifts God has given you? Perhaps you need to pack a bag and take a little trip to see more of the world. What is God speaking to you about enjoying the life He gave?

Prayer: Thank You, God, for the gift of nature and all Your creations. Thank You that created life for our enjoyment. You have given generously all things. I have a responsibility to listen to You so that I can receive the direction I need to go in life. May I be obedient.

Reflective scripture: "And God said, 'See, I have given you every herb that yields seed which is on the face of all the earth,

and every tree whose fruit yields seed; to you it shall be for food. Also, to every beast of the earth, to every bird of the air, and to everything that creeps on the earth, in which there is life, I have given every green herb for food; and it was so.' Then God saw everything that He had made, and indeed it was very good. So the evening and the morning were the sixth day" (Genesis 1:29–31 NKJV).

Acorn in My Pocket

Toward the end of August, I always get anxious for fall to arrive because it is my favorite time of the year. I love the crunch of leaves, the pumpkins on door stoops, the coziness of a warm sweater, and an excuse to drink hot chocolate. On this day, my head is down as I nonchalantly walk my dog down the familiar road of my neighborhood. There it is, taking me fully by surprise, the first acorn of the season, complete with its little brown cap and twiglike stem covering its partial green body. Excitement fills me each year when I see the acorns separated from the trees, announcing that fall is soon to be. I bent down and smiled as I placed the acorn in my pocket.

I traveled on and noticed a neighbor in his yard, and I stopped to say hello. He shared how difficult things were in his life at this time and that not much was bringing him joy. I felt the tiny acorn in my pocket and said that I, too, sometimes felt this way, but I thought it important to keep my eyes fixed on God. Instead of looking around us and seeing all the devastation, war, pandemic, sickness, and day-to-day sadness, I thought looking up was a better alternative.

Not everyone gets it, I know, regarding my reference to "looking up." I do not diminish anyone's burdens or hardships. I, too, have had them, but Jesus reminds us that He cares about the slightest details of our life. He even knows when one acorn has fallen from a tree. God sees each of us and wants our hope to be in Him. He who loves us unconditionally and eternally will never forsake us no matter how bad life might get!

God wants to journey with us, and He will if we take the time to invite Him to join us. If we are down and discouraged, brokenhearted, feeling forgotten, or just enjoying a walk and finding an acorn, God will join us! Please do not forget to invite Him to journey with you. He understands anything we might be going through. After all, He was human too and had similar experiences.

The little acorn sits atop my shelf, reminding me of the approaching cooler weather, crisper air, a chance to once again cozy up by the fire and another opportunity to relax, knowing that God has us all in the palm of His hand. Oh, yes, He does!

Prayer: Thank You, God, for little acorns, sweet neighbors, the smell of fall, cozy sweaters, a chance to relax and to trust in You, and for being able to "look up" even when life does not make sense.

Reflective scripture: "For the Lord will be your confidence and will keep your foot from being caught" (Proverbs 3:26 NKJV).

Do Not Hold Your Breath

I watched from my pew as his blue sneakers quietly skimmed the red carpet. He was a little guy on a mission, a mission of lighting the Christ candle. It was a dim kind of day outside, with drizzling rain falling. Inside, peace could be found as my mind wandered a bit while the Scriptures were being read. I was focused on the blue sneakers and the contrast of the red carpet. My mind began writing this devotion. In order to remain focused on the service, I wrote two words of reference, "blue sneakers" and "red carpet." I will revisit these words later.

There was no real significance regarding the blue sneakers, just that a young boy was wearing them that day as he performed his acolyte duties. The red carpet was his path to his destination, the Christ candle. We all held our breath as we waited for the moment when the candle and wick finally were as one. Holding our breath… how long would it take? I have seen it take forever it seems, but today, the wick and flame are ignited quickly. Celebrating in my heart the accomplishment of the young boy, I exhaled and settled into my pew for the sermon.

Later, as I type this, I am reflecting on the times in our lives we hold our breath, waiting for God to answer a prayer or show up in our lives and in our churches. Or perhaps we are holding our breath and praying that He will ignite the flame within that has seemed to have gone out with the wind.

God will move. Just as the blue sneakers glided on the red-carpet path toward the candle, God will show up and light the flame where He needs to. You do not have to hold your breath. In fact, you probably need to breathe more slow, long breaths. Everything is going to be okay.

Prayer: God, I thank You for breathing life and breath into me. Remind me that everything in my life is centered on You. Through You, I can accomplish all things. Calm my spirit as only You can, dear Lord. Amen.

Reflective scripture: "Let everything that hath breath praise the Lord. Praise the Lord" (Psalms 150:6 NIV).

Judge Not

When someone comes to our minds to pray for regarding a particular behavior, does that mean we are being judgmental? For example, let's just say I'm going to pray for so-and-so because they are dealing with alcoholism. Now, I may know that person well and know it to be true that they drink to the point of intoxication on a regular basis, but that does not mean I have the right to judge their behavior? That is God's job.

We all sin. We have forgiveness and redemption through God's grace. The Bible says so. The Bible also says, "He that is without sin, cast the first stone" (John 8:7b KJV). No, we do not judge the behavior or the individual. We pray for them and let God do the rest. Our job might be to help the individual find help, talk with them, pray with them, but do not judge. After all, we were not born wearing a robe or with a gavel in our hand.

Some people may go on to become judges, and our world needs those people. But I am talking about judging in the form of a verb, not a noun like a profession. Pray, yes; judge, no!

The next time someone comes to mind to pray for, pray for the individual, not the behavior. Think of them standing clean before Christ. In your mind, see God wipe away old pain, hurt, and challenges of that individual. Hopefully, you yourself have been the recipient of the prayers of others along life's way. I know I have, and I am grateful for those who did not judge me. We all make mistakes, and we sometimes create earthly jails for ourselves that God never intended us to be locked in.

Forgiveness is for all. That is right—for *all!* We may suffer the consequences of our sins, but God rewards those who turn back to Him. So lay your robe and gavel down as you kneel in prayer.

Prayer: Father, forgive me for times when I have been judgmental toward others and their actions. Help me to pray instead of judge. Amen

Reflective scripture: "So when they continued asking him, he lifted up himself, and said unto them, He that is without sin among you, let him first cast a stone at her" (John 8:7 KJV).

A Falling Leaf

I watched from a comfy lounger seated on my outside patio in the early fall sun, a single leaf gracefully dancing down from the sky. So quietly it fluttered and rested contently on my deck, its purpose complete, or was it?

Fall is my favorite season of the year, and I love to feel both the acorns and leaves crunch beneath my feet and the crisp, fresh air of the holidays sneaking in. As I watched the leaves falling to the ground, my mind floated to the clouds above and a thought struck me. How many times have I fallen down in my witness for Christ? Most days are good, and I smile through the day, gracefully feeling the blessings of Jesus. Other days, I am challenged by my own lack of patience or moodiness due to life's frustrations, causing me to not be such a great witness for Christ. That always happens when we take our eyes off of Jesus.

But you know, even when we fall or fail, God still loves us. The fallen leaf reminds me that our purpose is never finished as long as we are alive and sowing Christ. His grace will sustain us through all seasons of life no matter the joys or difficulties. He understands our failures and times of falling. He is always there to pick us up. Thank You, God!

Regarding the fallen leaf I had observed, it was now beautifully gracing my outdoor space and giving me pleasure as it and others crunched beneath my feet. It still had purpose after all…just like us.

Prayer: Thank You, God, for the seasons of our lives when we can experience new things and new and marvelous ways of

You working. Thank You that even when we fail and fall down in our witness, You still love us.

Reflective scripture: "To everything there is a season, and a time to every purpose under the heaven; A time to be born, and a time to die; a time to plant, and a time to pluck up that which is planted" (Ecclesiastes 3:1–2 KJV).

God Is More Than Your Feelings

God, how come nothing feels right?

Nothing? God said in my spirit. *Surely there are many things that are right. Concentrate on those things and be grateful.*

Well, what about "this and that?" You know…all the things that consume my thoughts? I pondered to God.

You are too concerned about too many things, things that have no bearing on you, my child, God spoke gently in my spirit.

Parked under a shade tree at my church right now. Sometimes you just got to pull over and pull out the pen and paper and let God speak. I hear the distant traffic noise, the cicadas singing, and the sound of my own mouth as I chew gum, but nothing can drown out the sound of God's voice in my spirit. My spirit feels a bit troubled because of things going on in the world. This particular day, I find solace here in my car, parked under a tree at my church and having a conversation with God about the ways of the world.

What would God say to you if you were to curl up in His lap? What is troubling you? Sometimes we carry burdens that God never intended for us to carry. Things we cannot control can lead us to feel anxious and overwhelmed. Ask God where He wants you to focus your attention at this time.

When nothing feels right in your life, trust that God is more than your feelings. Remember, there is no room for worry, sadness, and anxiety to coexist with God. Today, perhaps you could visit a sacred space and let the God of peace speak quietly to your spirit, giving you all that you need and filling you up.

Prayer: Dear God, when life does not make sense, let me rest in You. Remind me to focus on that which You have given me for the day. The rest, You will take care of in Your own time. Amen.

Reflective scripture: "Jesus said to him, I am the way, the truth, and the life. No one comes to the Father except through Me'" (John 14:6 NKJV).

Choose Wisely

You are a new creation in Christ! Yes, you! You have been since first accepting Him as Lord and Savior of your life. Trust that old things are *old* and ready to be discarded. The lies the enemy would like you to believe will rob you of your joy and peace. Joy and peace are fruits of the Spirit, and God intends for you to enjoy them! Savor them like a well-polished apple, each piece crisp and delightful, just like Christ. You are in Christ, and Christ is in you!

There is no longer room for anxiety, sadness, or need to control. Sometimes, these feelings have been with us for so long that we do not know how to react or live without them. God wants you to be free in Him. We get to pick what we want to fill up in our hearts and minds, so choose wisely.

God said to me one day in my spirit to "discard that which no longer serves Him or me." God whispered in my heart that I needed to grow up in Him and that He could not exist in my mind along with the simple gods of anxiety, worry, sadness, and need to control. You see, God is none of those things, and He will not compete with them. We need to toss them out of our being and make more space for God's peace and calmness.

We can grow up in Christ, meaning that we put our trust and faith in Him, but at the same time, we need to remember the simple childlike faith and adventure we had when we were younger. When we put on the mind of Christ, we let the spotlight of our minds and actions reflect back on Christ. We are called to reflect His peacefulness, calmness, joy, and fearlessness. Remember to choose wisely what will occupy your mind. I'll be right there with you attempting the same thing!

Prayer: "Let the words of my mouth, and meditation of my heart, be acceptable in thy sight, oh Lord, my strength, and my redeemer" (Psalm 19:14 KJV).

Reflective scripture: "And do not be conformed to this world, but be transformed by the renewing of your mind, that you may prove what is that good and acceptable and perfect will of God" (Romans 12:2 NKJV).

God Knows Just What We Need

Some days are like this: snow-covered trees, quiet walks, writing, receiving a red bird for prayer confirmation, a chat with a nephew who is in prison, and no shower until early evening. I am grateful for all that this particular day has held: a hat to cover my sensitive ears, a coat to keep my body insulated from the cold wet air, colorful gloves to cover my frigid hands, and boots to walk the snowy pathway that beckons my footprints.

Somehow, God just knows what we need. A gorgeous night sky with brilliant stars, the first sightings of the faces of spring daffodils, a lengthy conversation with a best friend, a warm rain, finding a bargain, a smile from a friend, clarity about a decision needing to be made, and watching a mixture of snow and flower blossoms blowing in the cold spring air—these are just a fraction of the wonderful gifts I have been given this week, simplicity at its finest!

How about you? What wonderful gifts has God bestowed upon you this week? Could you make a list of things that you know God has delivered right to you for your enjoyment? Gratitude is the beginning of a happy heart, I believe, and it is a wonderful way to end your day. Start this day by writing down four things you are grateful for having experienced. Watch your list grow and watch God work in your life!

Prayer: Thank You, God, that You know me so well. Thank You for showering me with Your creations and earthly blessings. Thank You for the opportunity to share Your love with others.

Reflective scripture: "I will praise you, Lord, with all my heart: I will tell of all the marvelous things you have done" (Psalm 9:1 NLT).

The Easter Dress

I knew the one I would choose. It was the bright-pink one with the yellow, green, and purple flowers, the one that buttoned all the way down the front with tiny pearl buttons. I watched as Momma took out her mother's sewing machine. Guilt filled me as she began to cut the hem so that the length would be exactly right for me. "Momma, are you sure?" I asked.

"It is okay," she said. Carefully, she cut away at the no-longer-necessary material, sewed up the sides to tighten the waist, and made the length just right for my little skinny legs. Soon I was twirling around the room as the dress flared out to my dance. Momma laughed and was pleased with her work.

It was Easter Sunday. Momma knew I wanted something new to wear to church that Sunday. There was no money for a new dress, so my momma had me go to her closet and pick out a dress, one of her dresses. I chose the one I had always admired her wearing.

Momma sacrificed. I was off to church to learn about Jesus, who made the biggest sacrifice for me and all people. My momma knew how extremely important learning about Jesus would be in my life. Jesus and pretty dresses go together. I think Momma thought so too.

Prayer: Thank You, God, for the many people in my life who have made sacrifices. Give me opportunities to sacrifice as well. Thank You for the greatest sacrifice of all, Your Son Jesus Christ, whom we serve here on earth. Amen.

Reflective scripture: "For God so loved the world that he gave his one and only Son, that whoever believes in him shall not perish but have eternal life" (John 3:16 NKJV).

Do Not Let Us Go, Dear Lord, Do Not Let Us Go!

Sometimes I just need to feel the hand of the Lord—you know, a clear feeling in my spirit that everything is going to be all right. Things in life are so disruptive from the so-called norm, and I am currently not even sure anymore what was normal. I have not heard a message of real honest-to-goodness hope in such a long time, but that does not change what I know to be true in my heart and spirit… and that is, God will never let me, you, or us go! No indeed, He will not!

Life recently has been like the whole world is on a roller coaster. I cannot put my finger on what the real problem is. Hard to do when people are fighting for this cause or that. We are fearful of not being politically correct, people are killing each other over such small matters, earthquakes, fires, weather, pandemics, and God has just about been removed from anything associated with the government.

Maybe we just need to feel Jesus hug us. Ever have that feeling? He hugs us through other people, I believe. Through kind words, physical hugs, smiles, and kind deeds—all are examples of God showing us love. Sometimes when we focus on other people's needs, our own needs seem to diminish. Our difficulties may not entirely go away, but fixing our eyes on others never hurts.

Perhaps someone today needs to feel a hug from God through you. Who has God put on your heart at this moment? If you are hurting, curl up and imagine God wrapping you up in His arms.

Wrap yourself in a cozy blanket and feel His peace for just five minutes. Remember, He will never ever let you go!

Prayer: In Your arms, I rest, dear God. Thank You for showing me Your love through others when I am hurting. Help me to hugs others who are hurting during these times as a way of displaying Your love.

Reflective scripture: "These things I have spoken to you, that in Me you may have peace. In the world you will have tribulation; but be of good cheer, I have overcome the world."

Material Gain

My dear friend of forty plus years just donated twenty tubs of material to a mission in Kentucky. Her husband thought he was doing my friend a favor when he brought the packed tubs filled with vast amounts of colored cloth to their home two years ago. Knowing how very much his wife enjoyed sewing and quilting, he had the very best of intentions. But they became a burden to my friend: pressure to do something creative. Instead, the rubber tubs sat in their house garage for two years due to life demands. She would look at the tubs over the years and long to do something creative, but nothing ever *materialized*. The tubs were destined for another purpose.

My friend began to have a deep desire to give the material away to a charity that was tucked away in the mountains of Kentucky. One day, after growing tired of looking at the "material gain" and listening to the nudging in her spirit, she packed her car and her husband's truck, and off they went traveling three states away with twenty tubs in tow.

When my friend shared her story with me, my mind traveled to the thoughts of all the material stuff we have gained in our lifetime, stuff that we do not need but perhaps someone else does. My friend was obedient to the nudging of her spirit to give the material away. She said it "hurt her heart because she loves to sew and quilt, but she hoped God would use it in that little mission area."

I am sure God has special plans for that material in the places tucked away in the Kentucky mountains. Perhaps the material will become bright curtains in a little log cabin or colorful pillows to brighten a dingy ole sofa or pillowcases decorated with crazy animal prints that will make a child laugh out loud. Maybe some beautiful pattern will become an Easter dress for some little girl. Just think about the endless possibilities of how those tubs of material will allow others to use their gifts of sewing and quilting to enhance the lives of others.

Only God knows what will become of the things we chose to give away. But rest assured, joy will be there for someone on the receiving end! May God grant you material blessings to give away today.

Prayer: Thank You, God, for multiple blessings of things and stuff to enjoy. Forgive me if I have too much. Let me be willing to share my blessings with others on this day. Show me what I can donate to help enhance the lives of others. Amen.

Reflective scripture: "Give, and it will be given unto you: good measure, pressed down, shaken together, and running over will be put into your bosom. For with the same measure that you use, it will be measured back to you" (Luke 6:38 NKJV).

Swishing Along in a Little Red Cap

His red cap was a bright contrast against the vivid blue sky of the morning. He trudged along in the cold morning air, looking like he belonged on a ski slope. Perhaps at one time in his life, he did. His body was older now—not debilitated, just older.

His walking pattern was very rhythmic. "Swish, swish, swish," his feet seemed to say against the cement sidewalk. Instead of ski poles, he was holding two walking canes and was bent over in his posture. In his eighties, I suspect. I spoke as I neared him on the opposite side of the street, but he had no interest in me nor my morning cheeriness, for he was focused on his exercise.

As I passed and stayed at a steady pace in front of him, I occasionally glanced back and imagined that he was using me and my dog as inspiration to keep moving forward. Even at a distance, I could see that his face was determined, and his feet seemed to will to his demands. "Keep going, keep going," I imagined him speaking to his body.

Each time my dog would stop to sniff at something interesting, I would glance back. The old man's red cap and determination began to make my eyes tear up. He had ministered unknowingly to my spirit that cold morning, and I had spotted him right away in his red hat. I admired his determination, his age, his focus, and his ability to move on despite any difficulty he might have felt. I said a silent prayer for him and will be looking for him in my walks. I want to thank him for inspiring me.

Today, perhaps you are faced with something difficult, something you are not sure you can get through. Keep your eyes focused on what will help get you through. Think about what or who your inspiration might be. Remember that Jesus experienced *it* all. Whatever your *it* may be, know that Jesus wants you to grab hold of Him. Just as the man was steady in holding his canes, Jesus will hold you up through it all. Grab hold of Him today!

Prayer: Thank You, dear God, for the times when You have held me up through it all. I thank You for sustaining me at all times, even when things appeared unsteady. Today, I give You all my worries, concerns, disappointments, and fears. You will hold me up despite any feelings I have, for You, oh Lord, are more than my feelings. Amen.

Reflective scripture: "The Lord is my rock and my fortress and my deliverer; The God of my strength, in whom I will trust; My shield and the horn of my salvation, my stronghold and my refuge; My Savior, you save me from violence" (2 Samuel 22:1–3 NKJV).

Seeing with Our Ears

The pianist calmly took his seat on the bench as the keys called for his attention. After a deep breath, the Christmas carol beautifully filled the church. I closed my eyes, looking forward to the talents of the pianist and the quiet reflection of the Advent season. During the playing of the piece, members had been asked to place their offering in the shiny gold plate on the altar table and to donate in a separately provided container any lose coins they might have, which would be given to a local charity.

The melody of "Lo, How a Rose E'er Blooming" filled the sanctuary. Suddenly, a loud clanging sound of something being continuously dropped filled the air interrupting my reflective time. "What was that?" I asked myself.

I knew right away where the sound was coming from. One by one, members filed to the altar and dropped their loose coins in the plastic jug. The *plop*, *plop*, *plop* was amplified by the microphones in the sanctuary and was a harsh, contrasting sound against the beautiful piano solo. My quiet time of reflection was about to turn into a bad case of giggles! But I managed to control myself, and God spoke to my spirit.

Was the loud dropping of coins so harsh after all? I thought of the coins and how they would help other people who were having difficulty in their lives. Times that perhaps were desperate and scary and not pretty or melodious. Times that were loud, and harsh, and fearful. Yes, truly the sound was disruptive, but my soul settled once again on the realization that sometimes in the quiet of our souls, the world rages on with its insensitivities to others, its desire to be right, and people are harmed and scared. But…the soul can be and should be at rest…if one knows Jesus.

No, I realized the coins being loudly dropped into the jug was not interrupting the beautiful piano solo after all. Instead, it was enhancing it. You see, if we can look deeper and search for meaning in things, we can begin to see Christ in all things.

The Christmas hymn ended with the sanctuary calm and peaceful as people had settled back into their seats. I was left with knowing in my heart that two things had just happened. We had heard a beautiful piano solo by our director of music, and we had heard the desperate cries of the needy in our community. May all be calm and bright, but may we see clearer with our eyes, our hearts, and our ears.

Prayer: Dear God, help us to see with our ears and listen to the cries of the needy around us. Thank You for Your gifts in abundance, for all things are from You, oh Lord.

Reflective scripture: "Whoever shuts their ears to the cry of the poor will also cry out and not be answered" (Proverbs 21:13 NIV).

Dancing on the Table

It is Christmas Eve morning, and I find myself catching up on some last-minute cleaning. The chandelier over the dining room table is getting cloudy, so I decided to have my husband help me take it down in parts so I could clean it up all sparkly. I proceeded to step from the dining chair onto the dining table. Never done this before as I had always used a taller chair instead to clean the chandelier. Carefully, I unscrew each piece, and my husband notices a small screw missing in one of the necessary places. I now know my quick cleaning had turned into a full-blown "husband project."

My patience with my husband's projects around the house is not the best sometimes, for I want to get the job done, and he sometimes sees other things that his crafty mind wants to fix at that given moment. So patiently—yes, patiently—I remain standing in the middle of my dining room table, clad in my Christmas pajamas and looking at myself in the mirror across the room.

Christmas music is playing throughout the house, and "Jingle Bells" comes over the speakers. I realize I have nothing better to do than dance! That is right! I danced right in the middle of my dining room table all alone with just myself. Before I broke into dance, I said to myself as I was holding the big glass portion of the chandelier, "Now what?" as my husband left me to get a new screw from the garage. Something came over me: it was my spirit that told me to dance.

I have never danced on a table before, at least not that I can recall, and it felt good. My husband came in the door just as I was nearing the end of my jingle bell ballet. I said, "First time for dancing on the table for me," pleased and feeling fun.

He just looked at me and said, "Just don't break the table!"

So does your spirit ever tell you to dance? It is okay to do so. The bible is filled with times of dance and praise. "Jingle Bells" might not get your spirit moving, but the important thing is to listen to times when your spirit is calling you to be fun, full, and free. After all, that's how Jesus would want you to be. Now, rock on!

Prayer: Thank You, God, for the gift of music and the gift of the Holy Spirit, who tells us to have fun and be lighthearted. Amen.

Reflective scripture: "A time to weep and a time to laugh, a time to mourn and a time to dance" (Ecclesiastes 3:4 NIV).

Peaks and Valleys

Turning sixty—what? Seems like yesterday I was on the front porch, living in Winchester, Virginia, dancing to the tunes of Archie on my portable record player. I guess at this age, I am supposed to be reflecting on life, and I have done a little of that recently.

Looking back, it has been a journey of peaks and valleys, and I am sure most people would say that about their lives. My parents divorced when I was thirteen—valley. My mom remarried a man who was different than my own father—valley and peaks sometimes. I attended ten different schools while growing up—thought it was a valley, but looking back, always being the new kid in school served me well. I am flexible. I wasted many years searching through life for all the wrong things—valley. I met Jesus and some wonderful friends—peak. I got married—peaks and valleys (ha ha, I can say this after thirty plus years of marriage).

I was never able to have children—valley, but I have terrific nieces and nephews, of whom I am very proud! I was led to return to school and get my BSW and my MSW at the age of forty-five—peak. I delivered the commencement address and even mentioned God during my speech—peak. I went on to work utilizing my degree, and God afforded me many opportunities to continue utilizing my degree and license for Him—peak.

Would I like to be younger? Some days I would, but I know that I am where I am supposed to be at this time in my life, reflecting, being quiet, and contemplating the next chapter, as they say, and feeling blessed. Even in times of aging and uncertainty, we can claim God's blessings on our lives. Peaks and valleys are all places where

God exists. He is in every phase of our lives just waiting to be invited to be part of the journey with us.

So what are your peaks and valleys of life? Take time today to invite God into whatever phase of life you are in. He wants to journey with you and guide your every move. He will hold your hand through all the ups and downs and will not let you stumble. If you lose your way, as we all do sometimes, He will be there to faithfully pick you up. Rejoice in that!

Prayer: Thank You, God, for walking each step of my life alongside of me. Thank You for carrying me, picking me up, and dancing with me as I live the life You have blessed me with. Amen.

Reflective scripture: "He will not allow your foot to be moved; He who keeps you will not slumber" (Psalm 121:3 NKJV).

Whom Do You Serve?

It happened one day while I was mindlessly scrolling through my phone. *Whom do you serve?* the voice said in my spirit. It stopped me instantly. I had been feeling some guilt these wintry days that I had been wasting so much time on my phone. Looking up various topics of interest, researching this and that, reading about other people's lives, the list could go on and on.

The convenience of instant answers had me almost compulsively picking it up, the small square black box of wonderment reminding me that I could find out about anything just by a few clicks of the buttons. The small voice in my spirit was reminding me that I had more important things to do than to mindlessly scroll through my phone. Scrolling can be relaxing somewhat, but are we really gaining anything in life by doing so? Should we not be spending our time on earth doing something more productive? These are questions with which I am often faced.

I enjoy communicating with family over social media, but I prefer a good ole phone call or a face-to-face gathering. I know technology has its place, but I think things have gotten a little out of hand with its usage. For me, I am disciplining myself to not rely on it so much for entertainment or fulfillment.

Lots of research have been done regarding depression and phone usage. Viewing other people's perceived happy lives, travels, successful children, accomplishments can cause us to become unsettled in our own lives. When we start comparing our lives with others, it does not settle well with our spirit, our mind, or our emotions.

God is a God of blessings, and I bet like myself, He has blessed you in impressive ways. Sharing your joys and sorrows, pictures of love and art are great for social media, and if you chose to do that, make it something uplifting. Give God the praise for answered prayers, ask for prayer support when needed, but limit your time. Do not let it replace interaction with others on a face-to-face level. It is convenient, I agree, but we would serve others better if we put some personalization in our service, and that is something social media cannot do.

Each time I pick up the phone now and am tempted to mindlessly scroll, I can still hear that "still small voice" in my spirit say, *Whom do you serve?*

Prayer: Forgive me, God, when I waste time with unnecessary things of this world. Forgive me when I compare my life with the lives of others. Help me to be filled with gratitude for all the goodness You provide me. Help me to spend my time wisely, for each moment is a gift. Amen.

Reflective scripture: "But if serving the Lord seems undesirable to you, then choose for yourselves this day whom you will serve, whether the gods your ancestors served beyond the Euphrates, or the gods of the Amorites, in whose land you are living. But as for me and my household, we will serve the Lord" (Joshua 24:15 NIV).

Do Not Weigh

The green tag fell out randomly from the stack of mail I had just picked up. The words on the tag were printed in bold capitalized letters: "DO NOT WEIGH."

Hmm, I thought, *wonder where this came from.*

I put the tag aside in a pile of papers that I keep for devotion ideas. The tag automatically made me think of *wait*—do not wait—but once I had a chance to ponder on the meaning of weigh, I concluded that perhaps God does not want us to weigh ourselves down with anything in this life.

It is our human instinct to carry around our worries and concerns instead of giving them to God. The older I get in my faith, the more I know how important giving our worries to God really is. The weight of life and all of its concerns have no place in our spiritual realm. Worries hurt the heart, the mind, the body, and the soul.

God tells us in His holy Word to lay our burdens down at his feet. As I reflect on the green tag, perhaps God was sending me a personal message that day, for I had been worried about a particular family member and a few other earthly concerns as well. When we are consumed with worry, it eventually catches up with us in our health, our attitude, and our interactions with others.

God's Word is wise, correct, full of wisdom and mercy. He tells us to leave our cares with Him for a reason. It is human instinct to want to fix things ourselves. Worry is not our friend. Worry is oppression and darkness and causes us to feel pressed down and compete with the fruits of the Spirit, which are just the opposite of worry.

We might have to practice giving our concerns to God. Sometimes we will have to do it over and over again until it becomes more of a norm. Do not worry, though. God is patient with us, and He waits for us to trust Him.

Prayer: God, You have given us so much in life to enjoy. Forgive me when I become consumed with worry and doubt. Help me to not weigh myself down with unnecessary worry that You are quite capable of handling because You are Almighty God. Today, I lay each burden down at Your feet. Amen.

Reflective scripture: "Give your burdens to the Lord, and he will take care of you. He will not permit the godly to slip and fall" (Psalm 55:22 NLT).

Run the Race Set Before You

"You want me to have a stress test?" I exclaimed to the doctor. *I do not want a stress test*, I thought.

I found myself in the emergency room one summer day after a *feeling* in my left arm, shoulder, and heart area would not go away. I had lifted two heavy pots and plants earlier that day and worked out in the hot sun, so I kept telling myself I was okay. Anyway, the *feeling* would not go away, so I used some good common sense that God gave me and went to the ER. My tests proved to be normal, but my doctor wanted me to have a stress test as a baseline.

So here I am, sitting in a waiting area, feeling stressed and concerned about passing the test. As I get my nerves under control and say a silent prayer. I look up and see a calming picture hanging on the wall of a beautiful white bird flying high in the sky. Instantly, I thought of the Holy Spirt. Yes, the Holy Spirit was right there with me, breathing inside me to give me the peace I needed.

I decided right then that I would reflect on that picture in my mind when I became anxious during my stress test. And do you know what? It worked! As the nurse said, "Just a few more minutes," and I thought I could not give one more second on that dang treadmill, I reflected on the Holy Spirit inside me and the scripture "I can do all things through Christ who gives me strength" (Philippians 4:13). As they shot dye into my veins, I imagined the white dove flying high in the sky, God taking my worries into His presence. God also provided a wonderful and caring technician that day, who explained each procedure before it occurred. I told her she was a gift to me and to others regarding her abilities and talents.

God sees you and will fly with you throughout this life. He gave us the Holy Spirit for a reason. God knew we would be troubled at times in our lives. I do not think we take the time enough to realize what a gift the Holy Spirit is to us. Pause now and contemplate this image of God within you. Grasp the truth of His ever-abiding presence.

The picture hanging that day was a gift to me. Reflect this day and recognize the seemingly coincidental things and ways that God speaks to you. If you believe that God is in control, then there are no coincidences in your life. The Holy Spirit is alive within you, and you, with God, have the ability to run the race set before you.

Prayer: Lord, the stressors of this life are many, but there is nothing that You have not ever experienced. Thank You for walking ahead of me and setting the example to follow. Thank You for the ways You encourage me to press forward and most importantly. Thank You for the gift of the Holy Spirit, who resides in me as a believer. Amen.

Reflective scripture: "Let us run with endurance the race that is set before us, looking unto Jesus, the author and finisher of our faith" (Hebrews 12:1–2 NKJV).

The Gift of Waiting

I had just helped a family member finish cleaning out my father-in-law's house. I was sitting in my car, ready to escape the emotional mindset of the day. Getting rid of other people's things is no easy task. I was the last to leave and about to start my car up when a feeling overcame me and spoke to my spirit, *Wait.*

I did not want to wait. I did not want to think quietly, and I did not want to have nightfall upon me before getting home.

Wait!

So I sat and bowed my head in prayer to ease the emotions of the day. I did not pray out loud, and I do not even remember if I prayed, but I remember closing my eyes for a few moments.

When I opened my eyes, there in front of me on the grassy lawn was the most beautiful buck with a full rack of antlers! I was amazed! He glanced at me before having a nibble of grass and then majestically walked across the lawn to his final evening destination, I guess.

I sat perfectly still and was dumbfounded. I remember uttering a *wow!* and then having a feeling of not believing what I was seeing. Not that I had never seen a deer or buck before, but it was the special moment that I knew I would have missed if I had not listened to that voice within. I had a destination that evening too, but God wanted to show me more, more that would brighten my emotional day and more of His creation, which is always a wonderful thing.

We must learn to recognize God's voice when He is speaking to us. We recognize it by spending time with Him in prayer, by reading the Scriptures, by listening to other believers, and by being silent. Thank God this day for the ways He speaks to you. And if He tells you to wait, be assured He has good reason to do so. Spend some time reading about Moses in the book of Genesis about waiting.

Prayer: Forgive me, God, when I am quick to rush through this life, oblivious to the ways in which You speak. Help me to slow down and be attentive to Your every move. Amen.

Reflective scripture: "After waiting another seven days, Noah released the dove again" (Genesis 8:10 NLT). Just think what might have happened if Noah had not waited on the Lord!

On My Knees in the Woods

It was a beautiful fall day, and I had spent the afternoon raking mounds of leaves in the woods nearby, preparing for my brother and his wife to visit from North Carolina. The excitement of seeing them gave me the energy I needed for the task at hand.

While raking, I began to think about a special bracelet that my husband had given me for our anniversary and that I had misplaced. Months ago, we had returned from a trip, and I realized the bracelet was missing while we were away. I started thinking that perhaps it was lost on the airplane. We called the airlines to see if anyone had turned it in, but no luck there. Anyway, I prayed to find the bracelet while I was raking and forgot about it after that.

While I was praying, I also asked God if I was on the right track in my life. As I was taking a load of leaves into the woods, I knelt and prayed for God to give me a sign that I was doing what He wanted me to be doing in life. I do not always pray such a prayer, and I believe we do not have to go around seeking signs from God all the time, for we must learn to trust Him, but for some reason, I needed to pray this prayer. I grew up with woods around me, so I find solace there sometimes, and it was a peaceful place to pray on this day. I did not spend a whole lot of time there and quickly got back to my raking and preparing for my family's arrival.

Later the next day, we decided to take our old Corvette out for a spin. I ran inside to get a jacket, and as I put one sleeve on, I felt something cold and odd. I panicked, thinking it was a worm or some sort of insect, but my panic quickly turned into praise as I pulled out my arm and looked inside the sleeve, and there was my bracelet that had been lost for months! I started praising Jesus. Yes, I did! My brother came running, thinking something terrible had happened, and he laughed with me as I shared with him my story and prayer in the woods.

You see, God really does care about every detail of our lives. He wants to reassure us we are His children, and He cares when we seek His guidance. Yes, the bracelet is a material thing, but God even cares about that, I believe. He knew it was a special gift to me from my husband. And God cared enough to reassure me that I was on the right track in my life.

Know that God will provide the same for you too. Seek Him out. Cry out to Him with your concerns. He will answer. Trust Him to do so. If you have a moment, take a quiet reflective walk in the woods, just you and God. It really is good for the soul.

Prayer: Thank You, God, for caring about every single detail of my life. Thank You for answering prayers and for prayers yet to be answered. Thank You for giving me the desires of my heart.

Reflective scripture: "Take delight in the Lord, and He will give you your heart's desires" (Psalm 37:4 NKJV).

The *Jesus* Sign

Five thirty in the morning comes pretty early for a yoga class, at least for me it does, but here I go down the road in the pitch-black morning with not another car in sight. It was a misty morning as well, making the wintry morning even more reason to have stayed in bed, but I knew my body would thank me later for stretching and keeping it toned as best as I could in my aging process.

Winding through the curves, cautious of deer, I look across a field and see a lit Christmas sign near a farmhouse with the simple words of Christmas: *Jesus*. The sign lit the darkness all around that morning across the open field. It brought tears to my eyes, for I know that Jesus lights up this dark world. I wondered how many other cars were privileged to see the sign that morning, or did they pay any attention to it and grasp the real meaning of the season? It spoke volumes to me that dreary morning. Jesus does light up the world!

Sometimes, we have to be the light of Christ for others. Many have come into my life over the years, and I am grateful for the light of Christ they have provided, helping me to find my way back in this world. We need each other, and everything we do points back to Jesus and eternity.

I wish I could have knocked on the door of the owner of that sign and told them what it meant to me that morning. It was one simple word but a powerful reminder and message of *Jesus* being all that we need. Be aware of the simple signs He gives you this day.

Prayer: Thank You, Jesus, that You are who You are: enough—enough to get me through each season of life. Thank You for the simple but profound ways that You speak. Amen.

Reflective scripture: "And she will bring forth a Son, and you shall call His name Jesus, for He will save His people from their sins" (Matthew 1:21 NKJV).

Picnic in the Car

Some of the fondest memories I have of my momma while helping to care for her when she became ill were picnics in the car. One particular morning, after a visit to the emergency room, we treated ourselves to ham biscuits and coffee from our favorite fast-food place. It was a hot morning, so I put my convertible top down, and Mom and I sat, laughed, and had breakfast in the car. Nothing like picnicking! We still had to drive across the mountain for her cancer treatment, so relaxing in the sun was a nice break after being at the hospital all morning.

I put on some good gospel music, and Mom commented that the sun "felt good on her bones." We ate our biscuits, and Mom ended up spilling her coffee, and I laughed as she attempted to clean it up with a soggy napkin. The laughter was good for both of us, especially Mom, who had been through a horrendous procedure already at the hospital.

She commented she was tired, and we both entertained the idea of her not going for her treatment, but she decided she wanted to go after fueling up on ham biscuits and coffee. Mom always did what was expected of her even when she did not feel like it. She was a wonderful example of pausing to have fun but getting done what needed to be done as well.

I have car picnics by myself now, but I think memorably on that morning with Mom—laughter, spilled coffee, ham biscuits, and sunshine. It does a heart good, especially when you throw gospel music in the midst of it all. Do something good for your soul today!

Prayer: Thank You, God, for the simple things in life. Forgive us when we try to complicate things instead of just relaxing in You. Help me this day to find You in all aspects of life. Amen.

Reflective scripture: "Beloved, I wish above all things that thou mayest prosper and be in health, even as thy soul prospereth" (3 John 1:2 KJV).

Missing the Mark

This morning, after getting dressed, the thought came to me, wondering if I had, at this time in my life, missed my mark. Ever felt that way, wondering if you are on the right path that God has for you, or if you are lost and do not even realize it? It tends to come to me more these days as I get older, for I know time is of the essence. I am not planning on dying tomorrow, but I know that God's work needs to be done, and as a Christian, I feel it my duty to do what God has commanded me to do. But what if we do not know what that is? What do we do then?

The older I get and the more I talk with some of my older friends, I am learning that it is okay to just rest sometimes. If you are like me, perhaps you have been a *doer* most of your life, and resting may not come easy. Growing up in my household, we kids were expected to always be doing something. Rare was it that we were not expected to be doing some of constructive value.

If we are a follower of Christ, He knows our hearts, and if our hearts are centered around serving Him, He will present opportunities for us to be used by Him. Sometimes we must rest up in order to have the energy for what is expected or demanded of us later. I know this to be true. I was attempting to make something work out for an upcoming fall season, and things just were not lining up or coming together no matter how hard I tried. God was not allowing my desires to come to fruition. He had his reasons, and it was hard for me to give in to defeat, but God knew that I would need to be available for my husband, who suddenly became very sick in the fall.

God knew I did not need to be distracted from other things, ministry or not. God wanted me available for my husband.

When we force things to occur in our lives, there will always be consequences to pay for our disobedience. Never forget that. Let God do the planning in your life. Go slow, for He will never have you miss your mark in life. God is a God of encouragement, not discouragement, so if you feel discouraged about anything in your life today, pause now and ask for forgiveness and do not listen to that negative thought. Replace the thought with *God knows where I am. He sees me, and He will continue to direct me to my* mark *at this time in my life.*

So let us get ourselves together, thank God for the opportunities ahead, and know that He is never finished with you until you reach His heavenly kingdom. Rest up and be excited about all that He has planned for you on earth and in heaven!

Prayer: Thank You, God, that You have me right on target. You will not have me miss my mark in this life. You are directing me, uplifting me, and sustaining me through it all. Thanks be to God!

Reflective scripture: "The Lord directs the steps of the godly. He delights in every detail of their lives. Though they stumble, they will never fall, for the Lord holds them by the hand" (Psalm 37:23–24 NLT).

A Bird's Nest of Blessings

"You were doing 54 in a 40 mph zone, ma'am. Are you late for an appointment?"

"Not really, sir. Just deep in thought about something. I know better, and I am so sorry."

"License and registration," the nice police office said.

Ugh! The flashing lights came out of nowhere. I was deep in thought on my way to my appointment, and my inventive mind of planning an event had taken over. You see, on my walk this morning, I happened upon a bird's nest. That is nothing great, you might think, but for me, it was an answer to prayer. I was so excited about that answer that I was totally unfocused on my speed. Not good, I know. The *warning* the police officer issued me was humbling, for I had been quite guilty. I would have liked to have shared my excitement of the morning with him, but I doubt he would have found it as joyful an event as I had.

The bird's nest was found on my morning walk. I had been praying about a big event that I wanted to do and was seeking confirmation from God. All the things were lining up regarding the event, except I did not have peace in a few areas about moving forward. The thought came to me as I was planning about finding a bird's nest to serve as confirmation. Now, as I have said before, we should not always need confirmation in a physical sense because if we listen quietly, we are able to discern in our spirits what God is telling us. But it felt okay to pray for a bird's nest, and I proceeded to be on the lookout for one.

I worked diligently in my yard one afternoon, just sure that God would bless me with a bird's nest, but He chose not to reveal one to me until I changed my plans regarding my unsettledness. After a few weeks, I cancelled the event plans and began to pray for God's new direction and peace. I became excited when He revealed a new plan to me, and on this particular morning walk with my dog, prior to the speeding issue, I was thinking of how to do the new event.

Suddenly, my dog pulled me to the opposite side of the street, and I reluctantly followed. As I looked down, there was a bird's nest at my feet. I suddenly wondered if I was dreaming and if I was seeing correctly, but as I picked up the small bundle of pine needles, various grasses, twigs, and foliage and placed it in my hand like a cherished gift from above, it was truly a bird's nest.

Only after I was obedient to that still, small voice of unsettledness within my spirit did God give me His blessings on the new plans, plans that were directed by Him and not me. God spoke to me through the gentle whispers of creation, and I had confirmation that the new plans were what He wanted me to do!

Do not speed through your day or plans as I was this morning. Slow down, walk in the sunshine, and let nature nurture your soul. There are blessings in abundance awaiting you. God will help direct and guide you as you seek His will. Ask Him for confirmation but be sure to quietly listen for Him to speak to your soul as well.

Prayer: Thank You, heavenly Father, that You love us so much that You answer prayers in a variety of ways. Help us to keep our eyes open to Your confirmations and our hearts open to Your peace about what to do in life. Amen.

Reflective scripture: "Let the heavens rejoice, and let the earth be glad; let the sea roar, and all its fullness. Let the field be joyful, and all that is in it. Then all the trees of the woods will rejoice" (Psalm 96:11–12 NKJV).

The Weeping Willow
Weeps No More

It all started about sixty years ago under the weeping branches of a willow tree. I was the little girl who would play in her sandbox and gaze at the nighttime sky. The weeping willow was my sanctuary, a place where dreams were made and life was discovered.

I had struggles like most people in life. My parent's divorced early, and that began the stages of shattered dreams. Daddy represented safety and love, and when he decided to leave the family, my little girl heart was broken. Family had always been important, but the circle was now broken just like that, snapped into.

Mom remarried. My siblings and I dealt with instability and moving every year to a new school and new town. My once well-adjusted childhood became a lifetime of trying to fit in and filling a loneliness inside. I let go of my dreams, but I did not forget the weeping willow tree. Was the tree to become a sign that my life would be spent under a rain of tears? Survival, school, and making the best of each day became the focus. I made many mistakes along the way, but thank You, God, for my grandparents and the guiding light that their religious habits instilled in me. It was what enabled me to persevere during hard times.

Forgiveness is the key that unlocks a hard heart. It is so easy to harbor ill feelings toward those who have done us wrong in the past. Forgiveness of self is also essential in moving forward in life and giving us true peace. We can only forgive if we understand the ways that God forgives us. The Bible says, "We are all sinners saved by grace."

God died on the cross for us so that we could have forgiveness of our sins. I had much to forgive in my past, and it was essential in order for me to grow in Christ.

Know that your scars of the past are stepping stones that ultimately led to the big picture created by God. Sometimes we get off track, make bad mistakes, and get carried away by self-made plans. The past will greatly influence the future, but one can overcome through Christ. We can return to the sacred grounds of childhood and remember dreams, goals, and carefree times when the world seemed perfect. God wants us to dream, and He longs to give us the desires of our hearts.

I return to the weeping willow tree sometimes in the quietness of my mind. I have a newfound respect for the tree's grace and beauty, a tree that has weathered the storms of life and is rooted and firmly planted in the faith of one's beliefs. I realize that I am now living the dreams of my childhood. Sometimes God is good enough to allow us to remember and to not be afraid to pursue those dreams. We have nothing to fear when God has ordained our dreams and goals. Keep your God-given dreams alive!

Spend some time in your heart asking God to reveal lost dreams to you. God places desires and hopes within us for a reason. Ponder those dreams. How will you make them a reality?

Prayer: Thank You, God, for dreams and for the gift of forgiveness! Thank You for dying for me and for allowing me to forgive others just as others have forgiven me. May my dreams be God ordained. I look forward to fun, laughter, joy, and a dancing spirit as I move through this life despite any hardships along the way. Amen!

Reflective scripture: "For by grace are ye saved through faith; and that not of yourselves; it is the gift of God. Not of works, lest any man should boast" (Ephesians 2:8–9 KJV).

Reflective scripture: "And be ye kind one to another, tenderhearted, forgiving one another, even as God for Christ's sake hath forgiven you" (Ephesians 4:32 KJV).

God Will Dry Your Tears

You think when you are caring for her in the quiet of your mind, *I will be okay when she leaves.* The thought of *she will be better off in heaven* is the only thing that seemed to provide comfort as she lay silently in her bed. Thankfully, we shared fifty-seven years together. I was the eldest of five siblings. I was the one to awaken at 5:00 a.m. to find her gone after we had all spent the night sleeping by her side. Silently, she slipped away, peaceful. She was like that, my momma.

I remember the hearse coming to take her away, the directors covering her in a beautiful quilt, my sister breaking down on the front steps, and the funeral director blowing three toots with his horn as we requested to signify "I love you," something "we girls" always did before departing from each other's homes.

I told Momma we would send her off like a queen, and we did! She deserved every ounce of goodness and blessing that ever came her way. She was a survivor until the end, and I have reflected on her strength many times since her passing. Nothing would prepare me for the feelings that would come after her passing. Feelings of the rug being pulled out from under me and a sense of being lost even when I had people around me. I know this to be grief. I have grieved before at various losses throughout my life, but nothing for me has been like the loss of my mother. But to live is to love, and to love is to grieve.

If you are grieving today due to a loss of some variety, come to Jesus, who understands. Losses come in many forms: through divorce, a loss of job, lost dreams, physical-abilities losses, a loss of a loved one—the list is endless. But God understands our weariness and tears. I remember a song entitled "Tears Are a Language" written by Gordon Jensen. Do yourself a favor and listen to it on YouTube. May your heart be comforted this day.

Prayer: Thank You, God, that You understand my grieving heart. You grieve alongside of me, and You understand grief as well. Thank You for the memories of loved ones and the knowing of seeing them again in Your heavenly kingdom. Amen.

Reflective scripture: "Blessed are they who mourn, for they shall be comforted" (Matthew 5:4 NKJV).

Reflective scripture: "The Lord is near to the brokenhearted and saves those who are crushed in spirit" (Psalm 34:18 NIV).

Reflective scripture: "You keep track of all my sorrows. You have collected all my tears in your bottle. You have recorded each one in your book" (Psalm 56:8 NLT).

Miracles Every Day

God gives us miracles every day. I am speaking mostly about small and seemingly unimportant miracles regarding life and encouragement—you know, the types of things we take for granted, like health, breath, nature, music, and laughter. My miracle today was the sweet and jovial woman I saw in the post office. She spread her joy throughout that place from the time she entered the door until leaving. A short amount of time, but she left an impression on me throughout the day, and I was still remembering her at the close of my day.

She moved with some difficulty in walking, but her spirit and joy were so fluid and smooth. When she entered the post office, it was as if the Spirit of God and joy had brushed all those standing in line. I do not know what it was about her presence, but her words radiated throughout the room, and a spirit of excitement filled me. It was the Holy Spirit moving in my soul, saying, *Yes, she gets it. You need some of what she has!*

I drank in the joy on her face and her attitude. My soul was thirsty and needed replenishing, and God showed up through her.

I prayed for that woman at the end of my day. I asked God to make her pathway smooth and that His spirit of joy would continue to shine through her so that people like me can witness Christ! I also prayed that God would give her all she needed in life, and I thanked Him for allowing me the privilege of observing one of His earthly saints in action! I want a small dose of that woman's sincerity and joy. It was genuine and came from God above.

May your miracles be overflowing today. If not, look to others, knowing Christ will show Himself in unexpected ways. Miracles do not have to be profound, but it is amazing when that happens! Sometimes in the simplest forms, miracles are revealed. Keep your eyes and ears attuned to His appearance!

Prayer: God, thank You for the numerous ways and miracles You provide that give us hope in this world. We could not exist without hope. Our hope is in You, oh Lord. There is so much to learn from You. You alone are a miracle, oh God. Your love, grace, goodness, mercy, care, support, and bigness are unending. Thanks be to God for ceaseless miracles. Amen.

Reflective scripture: "And in that same hour He cured many of their infirmities and plagues, and of evil spirits; and unto many that were blind He gave sight" (Luke 7:21 KJV).

Obey Me!

My dog ran away yesterday. Only for a few hours, but it was so frustrating the moment he escaped my grasp and slipped from his leash. Gone…off to find whatever scent his delicate nose had found. He emerged from the woods on occasion to allow me to glimpse his whereabouts, but for almost three hours, he was nowhere to be found. When I did spot him, he totally ignored my call and command. He had his own agenda. He had no concerns about my worry about his safety and the fact that darkness was approaching.

Why doesn't my dog listen to me when I call him? The training and schooling he had endured was nowhere to be found on this particular day. He had forgotten everything he had learned, it seemed, and was caught up in the delights of being free. He had escaped before, only to be sore from running the next few days, but the adventure must have been worth it to him at the time. It was only later, after a bath and giving in to sleep, that he realized that he possibly ran too far and too hard.

Aren't we like that in life sometimes? We have our own agenda and slip from the grips of God, get off track, follow our own scent of desires, and end up lost, frazzled, tired, and humbled. But just as I am there for my dog, frantically looking for him when he is lost, God is doing the same for us. God does not want us wandering too far away from Him. The repercussions of those actions can be long-term. I am speaking from a spiritual perspective. If not disciplined in our walk, scripture reading, fellowship with other Christians, church, prayer, and quiet time, we too can become subjected to wandering too far away. Remember, God does not move from us; we move from

Him. God is a constant presence, for He resides within you if you are a follower of Christ. Yes, we will blow it sometimes, but God will be there for us no matter what, for His patience is never-ending.

Be obedient to what God is commanding you to do this day. Listen to His voice speaking in your spirit and do what He is asking you to do. Remember to "go to school" each day and learn more about Him through scripture reading and prayer. Train yourself up so that when temptation comes knocking (and it will), you can discipline yourself to stay the course. Talk with other Christian believers who have wisdom and discernment. Being disobedient in any form to God's instructions is sin—not a good place to be. Life can be lonely and scary outside of Christ. May Christ be at home in your life today.

Prayer: Thank You, God, for life instructions that You provide through the Bible, Your holy Word. Help me to discipline myself to study, pray, and reflect so that I will hear Your voice when You instruct me in life. Thank You for never letting me drift from Your grips. Amen.

Reflective scripture: "All scripture is given by inspiration of God, and is profitable for doctrine, for reproof, for correction, for instruction in righteousness" (2 Timothy 3:16 KJV).

Trust God!

The truth and the enemy of this world cannot coexist. What do I mean by that statement? One evening, I was trying to rationalize why a particular project I was working on and excited about was not working out. I was discerning if the project was of God or of self—you know, one of those doubting times as to whether to continue a project just because it had become difficult or to keep moving forward, trusting God.

Doubt, discouragement, despair, feeling deserted are not of God, for God represents none of those things. God's makeup is peace, joy, love, encouragement, and if our *projects* result in all of those things or even make up a sum of those things, then I believe we should keep moving confidently forward.

Fear and doubt alone can be debilitating, but if those feelings are mixed with perseverance, faith, prayer, and God's guiding hand, then the truth is…trust God! Do not trust the enemy's words of defeat in your mind, especially when you have not even begun your *project*. It is a journey, and getting to the end of a God-given project requires trusting even when you cannot see the big picture. Quitting, I believe, just causes the angels of heaven to weep and to bow their heads, crying, "Oh ye of little faith" (Matthew 8:26). Sounds dramatic I know, but I want you to visualize that image of the angels of heaven hanging their heads.

Know that heaven is pulling for you! Do not trust the enemy and his lies. God's Word is truth, and if He is directing you to press on, do so even if you are afraid, anxious, or hesitant. You may feel negative things, but your actions can speak louder than your feelings. Keep pressing on, and more importantly, trust God!

Prayer: Dear God, help me to be brave, to have faith, to trust You, and to keep on!"

Reflective scripture: "And He saith unto them, why are ye fearful, O ye of little faith? Then He arose and rebuked the winds and the sea; and there was a great calm" (Matthew 8:26 KJV).

He Is Enough

I was a flight attendant once in my younger days. It was a very short career. I was the attendant who was in the bathroom, throwing up as the plane was landing. Yep, that was me! I was young, naive, anxious, and curious, but I had earned my wings, not knowing I suffered with an inner ear imbalance that caused me to eventually search out another career. I still continue to fly a lot to this day (I am on a plane now as I write this), but about twenty years ago, I had a panic attack on an airplane. Came out of nowhere, and to this day, my mind wants to go "back there" every time I step foot on an airplane.

I make special preparations prior to flying to manage my anxiety. Recently, prior to boarding, I was sitting in the terminal, wondering if I should take a magnesium vitamin to help me relax. As I was thinking about the supplement, God spoke in my spirit and said, I am enough. *You do not need anything else inside of you to calm you, for I, Christ Jesus, am enough!*

Well, that got my attention!

Now, I am not against medication for anxiety and have taken it as prescribed, and I am not talking about going against doctors' orders or prescribing a substitute for any medication. I am just telling you what was spoken to me in my heart. My point is that what I was hearing in my spirit reminded me I did not have to pray for calm or fret or worry about the flight or if I would have peace once I boarded (I always make out fine). Christ Jesus was with me just as He is with you at all times. Jesus is enough, and He is all we will ever need when facing times of anxiousness in this world. God likes to remind us that He is with us and very much alive and well!

On previous flights, my mind would not rest unless I had prayed, packed my Bible, prayed some more, took a pill or an extra supplement. Like I said, all those things are good and sometimes necessary, but they can never replace the One and only One thing we will ever need in this life, Jesus. Sometimes we attempt to ease our pain and discomforts in this life with various means only to have Jesus patiently waiting within, biding His time, knocking at the door, saying "Hey, remember Me?" God is enough for any and all situations, and do you know what? He costs nothing!

Think about the amount of money people spend to be comfortable in their own skin. Hundreds and millions of dollars, I am sure, and Jesus costs nothing! He is the one who sacrificed everything for us so that we can reap all the benefits. What fools we are to not recognize this, but…lessons have to be learned, growth has to be experienced, wisdom has to come before we can understand all this.

And now, as I write forty thousand feet in the air, I know God has many adventures ahead, destinations ordained by Him. He has great adventures ahead of you as well. Go with Him where He leads. It may be high into the clouds or walking on a dusty road. Wherever it may be, know that God wants you trusting Him and learning that He is enough. May He be a huge part of your journey!

Prayer: Dear God, thank You for revealing Yourself to my soul! Thank You for patience and healing and for Your divine appointments and destinations that You have planned for my life. Thank You for opportunities to recognize that You, oh God, are enough! Amen.

Reflective scripture: "Do not conform to the pattern of this world but be transformed by the renewing of your mind. Then you will be able to test and approve what God's will is, His good, pleasing, and perfect will" (Romans 12:2 NIV).

Dirty Shoes

There she sat in between the demands of three young boys. She took the time and patience to look one of her children in particular squarely in the eyes. She gripped his face in the cradle of her hands and kissed his forehead. She smiled with a gentleness of love in her eyes. *Why was he among the three singled out?* I wondered. No idea and not really important, just an observation. They were finishing up vacation, I assumed, as we were on a tram transporting us to the terminal for outgoing flights.

As the mom got ready to stand and disembark the tram, I noticed her dirty white tennis shoes. No doubt she had walked miles in them with her boys throughout their vacation. I am not accustomed to studying people's shoes, although I am a "certified shoe fanatic" by my own definition, but I did notice that her dirty, tired worn shoes looked attractive on her. They suited her just fine. My guess was that this woman had her priorities straight! She took the time to be present with her boys, and I am guessing her shoes represented miles of varied activities in which laughter, joy, tears, and happiness contributed to the stains that marked her once white shoes.

God expects us to have our priorities straight. He can help us to determine what those priorities are based on the life He has given us. Life can get busy and challenging sometimes, and God is like the shoelaces that hold it all together when things get hectic. But if we place Him first in all things, I believe He will enable us to step through puddles of joy even in the most difficulties of life.

Do not be afraid to get your shoes dirty, for life is not perfect, and when someone stops long enough to cradle your face and give you a kiss on the forehead, be grateful. A hug, a kind word, and forgiveness go a long way in this ole world. Now let's go get our shoes dirty!

Prayer: Thank You, God, for times of slowing me down, times when I need to get my priorities straight and focus on what is truly important in this world. Thank You for the gift of family and for the vacation and adventures. May I be the one who takes the time to tell someone today how very much I love them.

Reflective scripture: "And be ye kind one to another, tender-hearted, forgiving one another, even as God for Christ's sake hath forgiven you" (Ephesians 4:32 KJV).

Sit Down, Cody

She was a rambunctious little girl. I could see her dad's patience was being tested. She ignored his pleas to get down off the wall, to stop running, to stop dancing, to stop her constant singing, or whatever else her energetic little body felt like doing. Suddenly, one direct sentence spiced with sternness got her attention: "Sit down, Cody!"

She listened. She sat down with her energy now contained, behaving as others desired her to do. I could identify with the little's energy. I remember having so much childlike energy in me growing up that I wanted to dance, sing, jump, and wiggle all at the same time!

Jesus allows only so much diversion from Him in life. Sometimes He might have to seemingly scream at us in various ways to come and "sit down" with Him. He has things He wants to tell us, to reveal to us, to experience, and we will never know what those things are unless we sit quietly with Him throughout life.

We get excited and overwhelmed and caught up in our own agendas that we sometimes ignore His demands of siting down. There are consequences in ignoring His voice just as there would have likely been consequences for the little girl if she had not obeyed her dad's voice and command to sit. Her sitting perhaps kept her from getting hurt as she played and danced closer and closer to the edge of the fountain filled with water.

Sitting before our Father helps to keep us from danger also. It is to our benefit to sit quietly before Him before we contemplate our next move in life. Hopefully, dancing, singing, wiggling, and jumping will be part of the journey no matter our age!

Prayer: Dear God, help me this day to manage my emotions and energy. Help me to discipline myself to the hearing of Your voice in the various ways that You speak. May I be grateful for the times of quiet as You speak to my spirit and help me on a daily basis. Amen.

Reflective scripture: "She had a sister called Mary, who sat at the Lord's feet listening to what He said" (Luke 10:39 NIV).

Butterflies, Bubbles, and Bird Nests

It had been a busy day…getting ready for summer—scrubbing outdoor furniture and windows, planting flowers, and hauling out all the summer decorations as well as hanging the American flag in preparation of Memorial Day. Sometimes I wonder why bother with all this, meaning it takes so much of my time. "But what would I be doing otherwise?" I ask myself.

As I was packing the car to transport items to our summer place, I saw a beautiful butterfly resting on my driveway in the sun. I approached it, thinking it was injured. Just as I reached for it to see if it was wounded, the butterfly took off high into the trees—just resting. I paused, taking in the moment, and as tired as I was, it was inspiration enough to go on.

At the beach, I felt as if I was drowning in work that needed to be completed. I began to feel overwhelmed at having to get ready for summer and prepare for company and entertainment. As my husband fired up the power washer for the washing of the house, I took a break from my planting and leaned against the brick wall. I closed my eyes, taking in the sunshine. Upon opening my eyes, tiny bubbles from the soap of the house washing floated high into the air, so graceful, slow, and tiny. The bubbles somehow caused me to slow down and just take in the moment of sunshine and blue skies. My heart seemed to say, "Ah."

Soon it was time to rehang my wreath on the door that had blown off in a storm, and my neighbor had returned it, placing it on a chair outside my patio. As I picked up the wreath, I saw a beautiful bird's nest tucked snuggly between the green and white ribbons.

I remembered thinking I saw what appeared to be an eggshell in front of the doorway as I came into the house earlier. I realized what had happened. The wreath blew off my door during the storm, and the little egg fell out and was destroyed as it hit my walkway. My heart was touched as I examined the sweetness of the beautiful nest. A momma bird preparing a home for her loved one. I imagined the many trips she made back and forth, back and forth, preparing the home with just the right twigs, grass, and pine needles. How tired she must have grown.

I hung the wreath, leaving the sweet little bird's nest in place. I swept up the shattered eggshell and then took the time to think about momma bird and myself preparing our homes for those we love. Everything does not need to be perfect, and keeping things simple is always a good idea…just like butterflies, bubbles, and bird nests.

Prayer: Thank You, God, for the simplicities of nature. Thank You for refreshing our souls and giving us all things to enjoy. Thank You for all the goodness You allow us to experience through You, my heavenly Father. Amen.

Reflective scripture: "This is the Lord's doing; it is marvelous in our eyes. This is the day which the Lord hath made; we will rejoice and be glad in it" (Psalm 118: 23–24 KJV).

Candy Apple Lotion

Traveling by car to meet my sister for a long weekend together, my head entertained several ideas of what the weekend might entail as I sat behind the steering wheel for the seven-hour journey. I had booked a bed-and-breakfast and was excited. The pictures on the Internet looked lovely, relaxing, and inviting. Wonderful big beds to relax in; beautiful, rich old linens; an eclectic mix of antiques; and a home-cooked gourmet breakfast. *Ooh*, I thought suddenly, *wonder what kinds of luxury soaps and lotions they will offer?* I purposely did not pack my own lotion and soaps for the pure joy of trying something new and perhaps exquisite.

As I arrived earlier than my sister, the owner greeted me with all the excitement of a gracious host. I was shown around the property and thought, *Okay, not exactly what I expected*, but it had a certain amount of charm to it.

As I was led to our room, I was greeted by a historical array of lamps, pull-chain lights, butterfly wallpaper, creaky floors, and the tiniest bathroom I think I have ever seen. *Where are the pretty soaps and lotions?* I asked in my head.

Upon entering our bedroom, a tall poster bed with beautiful linens and draperies was what I first noticed. Old dressers lined the walls and the strangest chandler that looked like an upside-down vase graced the ceiling. A sweet lamp and small table occupied one side of the bed, and I knew it would be a great spot to lay my writing journal and pen.

Unpacking took only a small amount of time, and a bathroom break was calling. I entered the small chamber, complete with a compact shower, tiny sink, and commode. Disappointment began to approach, but really, what more could we need for the weekend? Pretty soaps and lotions were not to be found. A generic bottle of liquid soap sat on the shower shelf. Nothing wrong with that, but it was just not what I expected. A tiny basket on the back of the toilet contained used shampoo and conditioner and a small pink bottle of half-used lotion labeled, "Winter candy apple." It was June.

Expectations—we all have them. Sometimes it truly does benefit us to lower them in order to just relax and accept things as they are. Lowering my expectations of pretty soaps and lotions is certainly small compared to major life events. We sometimes will be challenged with serious matters and disappointments. We need Jesus to handle those things, and we can expect Him to handle everything we will ever face in life. We never have to doubt Him. He may even surprise us along the way and go beyond our expectations, or He may offer up winter candy apple lotions and expect us to be grateful.

I want you to know that I slathered on that winter candy apple lotion every day of my stay. The last morning there, I smoothed it on again for the last time, knowing in my heart that there are worse things in life than smelling like a candied apple.

Prayer: Thank You, God, for helping me to lower my expectation when necessary. Thank You too for the many surprises in life that You grant us because You love us so very much. Thank You for far exceeding our expectations and blessing us beyond comprehension.

Reflective scripture: "Finally, brothers and sisters, whatever is true, whatever is noble, whatever is right, whatever is pure, whatever is lovely, whatever is admirable, if anything is excellent or praiseworthy, think about such things" (Philippians 4:8 NIV).

It's All God

Driving for seven hours will make your eyes see double sometimes. That is why taking small breaks is always a good idea.
Prior to one of those breaks on a recent road trip, I came upon a
tractor trailer cab cruising down the road at top speed due to not
carrying a load behind him. The cab was shiny, black, and clean.

What caught my eye from a distance were the words printed
on the back of the cab in pretty gold cursive writing: "It's All God."
"Wow," I said to myself, "what a great message!" The words could
apply to anything in life, and if God is in it, then all the better!

I also thought these words needed to be made into a banner and
wrapped around the world right now. With all the wars, pandemics,
economic decline, hunger, homelessness—and the list goes on—the
world seems to be struggling to find God among the *its* of life. But
God is in *it* all. We are not to lose hope.

I wondered what the driver of that cab was intending with his
message. He did not appear to be driving for any particular company
that I could see, *see* being the key word here because as I drove closer
to the big black cab, the writing became a bit clearer. "It's All Good"
was the message, not "It's All God" like I had thought I had seen.
Okay, I'll give it to him. The message was still good, positive and a
lighthearted approach to life. A catchphrase that I had heard before,
but I was disappointed that God was not part of the phrase.

Guess it was now time to pull over and relax my eyes a bit. I still
like my first sighting message better: "It's All God." Wonder if that
will catch on? God is in control, don't lose hope, and whatever your
it may be at this time in your life, remember, *it's* really all good with

God! Make Him a part of your day. And as we have heard others say, "God is good all the time. All the time, God is good."

Prayer: God, You hold all of the its of my life in the palm of Your hands. I invite You into my day, knowing and trusting that whatever comes my way, it will all be good and okay with You! This I pray and trust. Amen.

Reflective scripture: "Taste and see that the Lord is good; blessed is the one who takes refuge in Him" (Psalm 34:8 NIV).

Nightfall and Fireflies

I watched as the darkness snatched away every bit of light. The trees of the woods slowly blended into the blackness, only to become magically illuminated by dots of lights: fireflies or lightning bugs as I grew up calling them. I had a three-point view as I watched the night come upon this beautiful summer solstice evening, the longest day of the year. To my right was what was left of a partially sunset sky. Pinks and shades of blue hovered above the pine trees that were so still, they looked like they had been painted into the landscape. To my left was the final sky of sunset with vivid golds and oranges forming an archway over the tops of oak trees. The leaves looked black in contrast. It was a magical sight, but there is nothing magical about God. He is real and shows up all around us.

My ears were filled with the splash from my water pond, a cardinal singing nearby, a tree frog making the sounds of whatever a tree frog sounds like. I breathed deeply, wondering why I have not done this more often: watching nightfall. It was calming, and my eyes teared up at the beauty and sounds.

God is so good to give us nature and creation to enjoy. If you haven't observed it in a while, do yourself a favor and go watch the nightfall upon the earth. Life is busy and demanding, and God never intended us to be stressed and carry our burdens alone. See where your thoughts take you as you sit and observe the night sky, ponder, and wonder at God's greatness. I bet you can even remember being a kid and lying on the grass at night, gazing up at the starlit sky. Go ahead, take yourself right on out that door and lie in the grass. Let

God speak to your thoughts. Watch the nightfall and the fireflies' twinkle.

People are crying out to God to show up in this world. He is here, watching you and me, and knowing what we are doing every second. He shows up in various ways. We just have to take the time to be present and find Him. Nightfall and fireflies are a good place to start.

Prayer: Thank You, God, that nightfall can bring peace and calm even when my heart is weary and stressed. Speak to me as I quietly watch. Amen.

Reflective scripture: "The heavens declare the glory of God; And the Firmament shows His handiwork" (Psalm 19:1 NKJV).

Little Inspirations

Driving down the road one hot summer's day, I saw a car tag that read, "PUSHING." To entertain myself, I thought of the various things the tag might be implying. Had the person driving the vehicle had to push through many challenges? Had they pushed themselves through an illness, or was the purpose of the tag to inspire others? Possible *Pushing* was their last name, but that was no fun to imagine. I would never know unless I had the chance to pull them over and ask, but that was not going to happen.

About two hours later, another tag caught my eye that spelled, "LOVEMOR." I liked that one, and the message was loud and clear to me. Unless, again, it was the person's last name. I would again never know, but loving more is always a good idea.

On my way home that same day, I saw another random tag on a car that pulled in front of me during traffic. I laughed out loud to myself when I saw the word "ALLELUIA." The tag needed no explanation.

I was grateful for the little inspirational messages that God gave me that day, or maybe that is just how my mind works. I see a lot of personalized tags, but I have never seen so many inspirational ones as I did that particular day. Keep your eyes open for little messages that God gives you as you journey along with Him. I pretty much summed up my thoughts about the tags as this: keep pushing through life with Jesus, love more like Jesus even when you do not feel like it, and lastly, at the end of day, say alleluia to God!

Prayer: God, You know just what I need when I need it. Thank You for the various ways You encourage me throughout the day. May I be in tune with the many ways in which You speak and direct. Amen.

Reflective scripture: "Now may the God of patience and comfort grant you to be like-minded toward one another, according to Christ Jesus" (Romans 15:5 NIV).

Stay Awhile

Do you ever feel lonely? I do at times. I often felt lonely as a young girl growing up. I was often the new kid in school since I attended ten different schools growing up, so I never had much time to make many friends. I still struggle with feelings of loneliness at various times, but I know those are the times I need to be focused on my writing and getting closer to God. Loneliness, for me, can sometimes lead to creativity, just me alone with God and my thoughts.

I have wondered if Christ was ever lonely. Can you imagine what He must have been feeling the night prior to His crucifixion? He had asked His disciples to pray with Him, and according to Scripture, they fell asleep. I wonder too if Christ was scared to die? Loneliness and being scared are feelings that a lot of people in this world deal with on a daily basis. Just turn on the nightly news and you will get a small taste of what people are dealing with today. Those two emotions/feelings are the root of a lot of worldly problems, I believe—that and people needing Christ in their lives. I always think of Christ as strong and capable of handling anything that comes our way. He gives us the grace to sustain through loneliness and times of being scared.

Christ came to earth in human form, and He must have needed friends such as the disciples. His heavenly Father provided Him with the strength He needed to get through His crucifixion. God also provided Him with friends, such as the disciples. The night prior to His crucifixion, Christ asked his disciples to pray and stay with Him, but what do they do? They leave Him alone to face His death.

We need each other in this world. Jesus knew we would. Do not underestimate the power of presence. Your being with someone else who is hurting in various ways can be a true gift to that person. How many times have you needed someone to stay and pray because you have been upset, hurt, lonely, or afraid? Be grateful for those people. The disciples fell asleep, leaving Christ alone. How lonely. Be assured this day that Christ stays with us. He never leaves—never, never, never.

Prayer: Thank You, God, for the people who have been with me in times of difficulty. Thank You for allowing me to be a gift of presence to someone else. May we never take each other for granted. Thank You for never ever leaving me alone. Amen.

Reflective scripture: "Be strong and of good courage, do not fear nor be afraid of them; for the Lord your God, He is the One who goes with you. He will not leave your nor forsake you" (Deuteronomy 31:6 NKJV).

Daddy and the Airplane

As I sit back in my new Adirondack chair with a slight cool breeze blowing the evening sunset near, I hear various planes going by overhead. My memory took me back to a time when I was outside sitting on the grass on a wintry day with my brother by my side. I was about five years old. I have seen black-and-white pictures of that day with me in my winter coat, wearing a knitted hat and a scrunched-up face, and holding my left ear. "What is that up in the sky making that loud noise?" I asked my dad. I clearly remember my dad telling me it was an airplane. "Will we ever go on one?" I asked.

He laughed, and I remember him saying something like, "Probably not. It costs a lot of money."

"Where does it take you?" I curiously asked.

"Anywhere you want to go," Dad replied.

My dad was right. He and I never went on an airplane together. Six years after that incident, my dad left. He didn't die. He just left me and my siblings. Divorce, a hard thing it is, but my dad chose to no longer be part of our lives. I do not even know why really. I was devastated. His choice. It was hard to accept, but God's love finally healed the pain of loss.

I have been on many airplanes in my life, and often when I am writing outside, the roar of airplane engines in the sky provides background noise as God speaks to me, instructing me what to write. As I am transcribing this devotion, an airplane is flying over my house at 9:12 p.m. God is still speaking and healing, I like to think.

God helped me earn my wings when I was in my twenties. I had a very short career as a flight attendant. It did not work out for me for various reasons, and I still do not relish flying at times, but if you have read my other book *Fingerprints of God: 62 Day Devotional to Finding God in Ordinary Circumstances*, you know that God has given me many devotion ideas while seated on a plane, which has helped with anxiety while flying. Writing is a wonderful tool, by the way, for dealing with anxious thoughts. Just pick up a pen and begin.

Sometimes I still feel like that little girl on that wintry day all caught up in the words of her daddy, a daddy who left to have another life. I had no choice but to bear the pain. Once when I was flying, my mind drifted to all the other girls in this world and what tough situations they might be faced with and how the impact of their dads' loving words and presence versus leaving might have on them.

Like a passenger waiting to board a plane, I have waited over the years for my dad. I am still waiting. I forgive him only by God's grace. The doors have closed, I fear, and I may be left with unanswered questions, but God, in His mercy, has given me a greater understanding of His perfect love that is available to everyone, a love not like earthly man's love, for God's love will never leave or forsake any of us. No matter the weather, the circumstances, the battle, or the victory, God will never, ever leave, and He always shows up! People may leave, but God never does. He can take us to heights and places that we perhaps only dream about.

As a young girl, I could never imagine being on an airplane. I remember the first time I flew before I became a flight attendant. I was scared, alone, with no one to explain how an airplane took off, landed, or even what to expect, but I trusted. That is how it is with God. We sometimes—no, all the time—have to trust that His ways are perfect. He will carry us, lift us up, sustain us, and encompass us during the difficult and often turbulent times. And all the while, He is whispering to us and promising to never leave or forsake us. Thanks be to God!

Prayer: Thank You, God, for being everything that I need in this life. Thank You for loving and caring for me and remaining a constant. Thank You for showing up and loving me unconditionally. Mostly, thank You for being my Father. Amen.

Reflective scripture: "I will be a Father to you, and you shall be My sons and daughters, Says the Lord Almighty" (2 Corinthians 6:18).

Sista Giggles

There is nothing like having the giggles with my sister, and we have shared many of those moments over the years, giggles that make you laugh so hard, you can hardly catch your breath. From the moment my little sister was born, her giggles would make my heart jump with joy and still do to this day.

A recent episode occurred when we had booked some time together at a bed-and-breakfast. As we entered our room for the night, ready for a cozy bed, we noticed a large spider on the ceiling—not what I had paid for! My sister is terrified of spiders, so big sis had to come to the rescue.

Now, most bed-and-breakfast places are cozy quarters, so we were very aware of the people next door to our room. It was late at night, so we did not want to disturb them, but we had no plans to spend the night with a big spider hanging over our heads. I proceeded to find something in the room that I could swipe the spider down from the ceiling, which would enable us to quickly put it into spider heaven.

We found some dried cattails in an arrangement in our room, and I proceeded to climb on top of the bed and attempt to knock down our intruder. My sister, being of younger mindset, proceeds to video the whole scene. Really? But I climb on the bed and said out loud before swiping the ceiling, "In the name of Jesus!" I thought uttering those words would give me extra superwoman power! Instead, I missed my target and proceeded to fall onto the bed, laughing hysterically. I mean, we could not stop laughing, which caused our bedroom neighbor to commence making noise to let us know to please be quiet!

I can start laughing all over again as I type this! It was a comedic scene for sure all captured on video. My sister swears she is playing it at my funeral one day!

Research has proven that laughter increases the feel-good endorphins in our brain, which is a fabulous thing. The Bible even speaks about laughter being good for us. My grandfather told me once to never stop laughing; I cherish his words.

Today, perhaps you need to do something that makes your heart giggle. Sometimes we need to act like kids no matter our age. It can be refreshing to the spirit. How about you? What can you do today that will incorporate some fun and giggles into your life? Or perhaps you enjoy making others laugh. Whatever it is, now might be a good time to go and do it!

Oh, yeah, the spider finally made its way into spider heaven. I will spare you the details, but strike one up to my little sis who faced her fears!

Prayer: Lord, we praise You this day for the moments of laughter that You allow us to have even when our hearts might be hurting. You can be found in all things, and that is reason enough to rejoice. Thank You for the giggle moments You allow us to experience with both friends and family. Amen.

Reflective scripture: "A merry heart does good, like medicine, But a broken spirit dries the bones. (Proverbs 17:22 NKJV).

The Unseen Hand of God

Do you ever feel you are spinning your wheels in life, wondering what and where your next adventure will lead? Right now, I find it a challenge to just be content. I seem to be looking for a new door to open, and all doors that I am knocking on seem to be sealed. In my humbled wisdom of walking with God, I know not to go hammering down a sealed door, so I wait. Waiting is hard, don't you think? I have always heard it is what you do in the waiting that can make all the difference.

Waiting, for me today, has included writing, doing a bit of yoga, listening to an old CD that my mom, stepdad, and family recorded many years ago. The song playing now is "The Unseen Hand." Wow. That pretty much sums up where I am in life now. I call it a God moment to have this particular song play while I am writing this devotion. I have never listened to this particular CD, and it is the first time I have listened to my mom sing since she passed away six years ago. Brings tears to my eyes as I hear her beautiful voice fill up the walls of this silent room.

What about you? Where do you find yourself these days? Are you content to be guided by the unseen hand of God? Trust and faith—those are the essence of Christian faith. God is guiding even when we feel like things are at a stopping point, like coming to a four-way stop sign and pondering which direction to take. Be assured that God wants to be a part of every step of your life. Even when you are in a holding pattern like an airplane, circling and waiting to land, God is ever busy taking you somewhere. His plans never lead to nowhere, for His plans are for us to prosper and to give us hope for the future.

So go on with your day and know that God will open just the right door at just the right time in your life. I will be right there with you, trusting God every step of the way and waiting for His perfect timing, and watching His unseen hand at work. Watch for His beautiful artwork to show up in your life, artwork that could only be painted by God's amazing hands.

Prayer: Father, forgive me when I become restless and unsettled in life. Help me to see Your hand at work while I rest, wait, and trust, knowing that Your destination for me will be perfect.

Reflective scripture: "My soul, wait silently for God alone, for my expectation is from Him" (Psalm 62:5 NKJV).

❧ ❧

A Ray of Sunshine

Her dress was the color of a glorious sunset, but she looked like sunshine as she stepped out of her home this bright summer morning. With coffee in hand, she carefully stepped down in her coral dress and strappy shoes, ready for her day. My neighbor looked so pretty, I just had to shout compliments to her from the street. "Thank you," she sweetly replied.

I smiled as I walked on toward my house, knowing my neighbor was likely headed to work and would probably receive many more compliments that day. I, on the other hand, this morning had thrown on my workout clothes from yesterday, barely combed my hair, had applied no makeup, and was zipped up in a jacket…braless. Yes, I just said that. I really should try to do better sometimes, but my only chore this morning was walking my dog, and I was okay with that.

Seeing my neighbor was really the start of my day. She truly did cast a bright light on the morning. She was pretty, well put together, and judging by her appearance, no one would have guessed her story. I knew part of her story. Her story was one of pain and struggles. I had watched and prayed for her and her family from afar over the last few years. I hoped this morning that her bright appearance had to do with her refreshed outlook on life after going through so much uncertainty. She looked picture-perfect.

Many times, we judge people by their outward appearance. How unfair. How shallow of us as a people to live among hurting people and not bother to get to know them because everything in their life appears fine. I have been judged over the years. I bet you have too. It does not feel good, does it? Perhaps if we took the time to compliment people more, pray for our neighbors who are hurting, or even reach out to a stranger, we, too, could be the ray of sunshine that someone else needs. Jesus commands us to pray for others, follow His commandments, help the homeless, feed the hungry, and be the light to the world—in other words, reflect Him. I'm going to get my act together today and make it a goal to go spread some cheer if I can. But first, I better find my bra! Lordy, some days are just like that. Sorry!

Prayer: Lord, help me to be a ray of sunshine to someone's life today. Give me opportunities to spread cheer and encouragement wherever Your path may lead. Amen.

Reflective scripture: "Let your light so shine before men, that they may see your good works, and glorify your Father which is in heaven" (Matthew 5:16 KJV).

Tommy

He was always a bit disheveled in his appearance. When I first met him, I wanted to scrub him up a bit and buy him some new clothes, especially a coat, but that would have been insulting to him. He lived alone and was perfectly capable of taking care of himself. He was a bit odd, you might say, in his character, and he always wanted to tell me a joke…a dirty joke.

The first time he told me a joke, I laughed a bit just to satisfy him, and it was funny, but the more I encountered him, the more I wanted to learn more about his life, jokes aside. He was guarded in sharing, but little by little, he revealed more. He seemed to be alone in his life and spoke of distant family. Months would go by before I would see him. When I did see him again, he wanted right away to tell me a joke. "Okay," I said, as long as it isn't a dirty one!

This took him by surprise, and he paused a minute, and I could tell his brain was in rapid fire to produce an appropriate joke. He couldn't, so I just proceeded to ask him what he had been up to. He shared with excitement about having doughnuts and coffee outside a convenience store with a friend recently and talked about their various topics. I could tell the time with his friend had been meaningful.

You see, sometimes it's all about the open-ended questions we ask people that cause them to open up a bit. People are hungry for conversation, I believe, hungry to talk about themselves and their lives. We get so caught up in our own lives that we fail to hear the cry of those who are longing for something, something they don't even know is missing.

People miss different things in their lives, depending on the season they are in. As we age, our needs become different. People, friends, and family die, move on, and relationships wain in and out like a thread through a blanket. We ride the roller coaster of life and try to do it alone, but it is God and others who help us get through difficulties.

What are you in need of today? Can you ask someone to help you? Will you be that someone to a friend or a total stranger who needs a listening ear? Get quiet for a few minutes and ponder what God wants you to do regarding the people you encounter.

Today, I overheard my aforementioned friend speak to no one in particular. He did not have a clue I had overheard him, but he said, "Tommy here, listening." It was a sweet reminder that even Tommy, who was mostly a loner, had the time and desire to listen to others. May it be so with you today.

Prayer: God, thank You for enabling me to encounter others who need encouragement. Thank You to those who have taken the time to listen and have been instrumental in leading me to You. May the words of my mouth always be an encouragement to others. Be in constant control of my life, and may I always reflect Your love in all that I do and speak. Amen.

Reflective scripture: "Let the words of my mouth, and the meditation of my heart, be acceptable in thy sight, O Lord, my strength, and my redeemer" (Psalm 19:14).

H-O-P-E

Give me an H, an O. Give me a P and an E. Wha-da-ya got? *Hope!* What gives you hope these days? In a world currently filled with violence, pandemics, economic shortages, and churches splitting up, I wonder where people's hope rests.

For me, hope is in that cup of coffee I shared with a friend today. Hope is in the smile and friendly exchange received from my dog's groomer. Hope was found in that delicious massage I received, knowing that ease would come to my aching muscles.

As I had my quiet time and reflected on the day by my pond, hope was found in the Scriptures, in nature, and in the joy of water splashing in my pond. Hope was in the bird's song serenade coming from a high treetop, and hope was on the whispers of the gentle breeze. I am not blind to all the disruptions in our world today, and I truly know where real hope lies. Real hope and rest are found in Jesus. He is the stabilizer when life seems out of hand. He is our rock and our hope.

God wants us to be filled with hope. In order to find balance, we have to take our eyes off the worldly happenings of the day and refix them on Christ. It's easy to become overwhelmed in today's world, but hope is there. It can be found in the small things that God provides throughout our day. It really is our choice as to what we will focus on. God gives us free will, free to make decisions on our own. With those decisions, consequences will follow. Better to have Jesus a part of those decision so that we can remain hopeful in Him.

We can trust Christ and all that He has promised in our lives, so go on out and face the world today. Look intentionally for hope. It's there. Just listen, look, and relax. God's got this!

Prayer: Thank You, God, for the Scriptures, which are filled with Your messages of hope. Help me to fix my eyes on You, the sustainer of the universe! Amen (see if you can commit one scripture verse below to memory to help you focus on hope through Christ).

Reflective scriptures:

> **Now may the God of hope fill you with all joy and peace in believing, that you may abound in the hope by the power of the Holy Spirit. (Romans 15:13 NKJV)**

> **"The Lord is my portion," says my soul, "Therefore I hope in Him!" (Lamentations 3:24 NKJV)**

> **I wait for the Lord, my soul waits, And in His word I do hope. (Psalm 130:5 NKJV)**

> **Now faith is the substance of things hoped for, the evidence of things not seen. (Hebrews 11:1 NKJV)**

Secret Squirreling

My little brother has a name for people who gather in private conversations that exclude others in the room. He calls it "secret squirreling." I do not know how he came up with the name, but it ticked me the first time I heard him refer to it. Of course, it was I and my sister who were "secret squirreling" at the time, so he felt comfortable calling us out. We didn't intentionally leave him or anyone else out of the conversation, but he took offence to it.

Leaving others out does not feel good. I know this to be true, and perhaps you do as well. "Secret squirreling" can lead to gossip even though it might not have been ones first intention. I am careful not to "secret squirrel" particularly around those whom I love. When others approach, it is probably a good idea to invite them in on the conversation if appropriate. When it comes to God, he doesn't hide things or keep secrets from us.

We need to be careful what we say regarding others. God convicts me of this at times. I really do attempt to see the good in all people, but when people have hurt us, it can be difficult but possible to forgive. We are wise to guard our thoughts and our tongue. The Bible speaks strongly regarding the power of the tongue and the potential harm it can cause (see Proverbs 18:21).

God desires to speak truths to us so that we can share good things with others. He longs to give us the desires of our hearts and to share the secrets of His promises. Yes, there are still things that God will not reveal to us on earth. We have to wait until heaven to know all things, His secrets. In the meantime, know that God is aware of the secrets of your heart. He forgives the wrong you may have committed or spoken, and He is the restorer of all things. All the secrets of this earth will be revealed in time, God's time.

Prayer: Father, please forgive me when I have spoken ill against another and gossiped. Forgive me for the wrongs I have done. I claim forgiveness through Your unfailing grace. Thank You for restoring all things and knowing the secrets of my heart. Thank You for refreshing me. Guide my conversations this day that they may reflect You. Amen.

Reflective scripture:

> **The time is coming when everything that is covered up will be revealed, and all that is secret will be made known to all. Whatever you have said in the dark will be heard in the light, and what you have whispered behind closed doors will be shouted from the housetops for all to hear! (Luke 12:2–3 NLT)**

> **Let no corrupt word proceed out of your mouth, but what is good for necessary edification, that it may impart grace to the hearers. (Ephesians 4:29 NKJV)**

No Pressure

Plop went the container on the countertop as the barista presented me with a delicious-looking iced coffee on this hot summer day. *Just want I wanted and did not even know it*, I thought to myself. I had missed my morning dose of caffeine and was looking forward to meeting a friend and enjoying some gal time.

Proceeding to the back room to find a table, I placed my coffee on the table and went to the ladies' room and returned, noticing a group of chatty women talking about prayer and discussing a book they had recently read. This seemed like a comfortable space I thought and proceeded to make my way to my table.

It was then I saw the four words: No Pressure, No Diamonds. I had to look a second time and study the message and then had an aha moment! What a great message, and I took it personally. You see, the owner of the little coffee shop had taken the time to write personalized messages on each of the cups she handed out. This particular day, I needed that message and did not even know it! I felt as if God had spoken to me directly. It was my own private moment of rejoicing in my soul.

I sat down and took in the space, waiting for my friend. "No pressure, No Diamonds," you see, spoke to where I was at this time in my life. Searching for a place to land. I felt pressured to be doing something and was struggling to find my stride. God does not want us to feel *pressured* in life, but He challenges sometimes us to sit still and wait for Him to work, knowing that He will produce *diamonds* in our lives that sparkle by His making, not our own.

God has a plan for each one of us. Trust that! He allows us to go through seasons so that we can experience different things. These things may feel unfamiliar and new, but they can be exciting if we just relax in the Lord.

I was personally so thankful to those four words on that coffee cup that I went to the owner and told her how much they meant to me. She smiled, and I knew she knew that God had worked through her to minister to others.

So remember, if you feel pressured in any area of your life, it is only because God is at work and has something amazing in store for you. Wait and let Him polish the areas of your life that need fine-tuning so that you will sparkle like a diamond, just like that barista in that small coffee shop.

Prayer: Thank You, God, that Your hand is always at work in my life through the pressures and trials. I trust You to work out the seasons of my life and cause Your light to shine through me. Thank You for the ways You use others to minister to our souls. May it be so with us as well. Amen.

Reflective scripture: "These things have I spoken unto you, that in me ye might have peace. In the world ye shall have tribulation; but be of good cheer; I have overcome the world" (John 16:33 KJV).

❧ ❦ ☙

Fallen Angels

It hurt my heart. It was a sad way to begin the day, seeing the dead baby bird on my driveway alongside its nest. The tiny feathers were so small, gray, and fuzzy, and tiny stick legs looked so perfect… yet they weren't. "Oh no," I said and looked up to see where the nest might have fallen, as if that would matter. I flipped the nest over, only to discover another baby bird hidden under the small mass of pine needles. My heart sank. In my weariness, I proceeded to the garage for a broom and dustpan as the ants were quickly circling in.

As I scooped up the two babies, my eyes could not believe it when I saw two more baby birds, now four total, that had succumbed to the fall. I studied them closely and was in awe of their perfect formation and short life span. I also thought the nest to be much too small for four birds, but I'm no momma bird. Momma Bird had been around during the accident because the driveway was scattered with white bird droppings. I am sure Momma Bird's heart sank more that morning than mine had.

I scooped them up and buried them together in my woods underneath the earth and pine needles. A baby pine cone marked their grave. I have tears in my eyes as I type this because the little ones never had a chance. I know sometimes human babies never have a chance either, and that is sadder than baby birds for sure, but God cares about all the fallen creatures, even us because we too fall and fail in life.

I can't make sense of the dead baby birds just like I can't make sense of a lot of things going on in this world right now. I do know, however, that we can do all we can to be effective where we are. I could only care for the baby birds by giving them a proper burial and by allowing the incident to hurt my heart. It is only when we allow our hearts to hurt that we will develop compassion for others, and that includes nature. We can slough things off, act like they do not matter, harden our hearts to life and events happening around us, or we can choose to care.

The birds will keep on singing, and nature will keep on creating, and God will continue to give us opportunities to care and nurture that which He has given…if only for a very short time.

Prayer: God, our hearts hurt sometimes by the cruelty we see and observe in this life, but we know that You give us more joy and peace than anything life can offer. Help me this day to do all I can to observe You at work through nature and others. Give me a heart of compassion. Amen.

Reflective scripture: "The Lord is gracious, and full of compassion; slow to anger, and of great mercy. The Lord is good to all: and his tender mercies are over all his works" (Psalm 145:8–9 KJV).

Momma's Voice

We hear a lot these days about gratitude. Some have suggested writing five things down each day for which you are grateful. I started this practice many years ago. No, I am not disciplined to write in it each day, but I do keep a journal by my bed, and I must say it is very therapeutic to reflect on the day and to end it on a positive note.

The first entry I have in my gratitude journal is "grateful for my momma's voice." Since her death six years ago, I no longer am able to hear her voice out loud, except for the saved message I have on my answering machine, where she called one evening prior to our going on a trip. "Hi, this is Mom. I just called to see what you are doing. I cleaned a bit today, and I'm a little tired right now. I'm getting excited about our trip. Talk to you later. I love you." Her voice rings a solid melody in my heart and soul, and it will never stop, and for that, I am grateful.

Sometimes, focusing on the positive and being grateful are not so easy. I get that, but surely, finding five grateful things in a day should be easy to write about or to reflect upon at the close of the day, and it is a heathier way to live.

I would sometimes tell my clients that having a positive mindset is like looking at a coin. One side is heads, and the other is tails. One side could represent positive and the other, negative regarding thoughts. But instead of flipping the coin and seeing where it lands, know that you have a choice in the matter. You can choose to be positive. Simple as that.

Carry a coin in your pocket or place one on your windowsill, reminding you of the choice you have. Start listing things you are grateful for and see how large you can get the number to be. I am up in the thousands now. It's fun to do, and the practice will enable you to truly see God at work.

I can't say my thoughts are always positive. I have worries and anxieties that I keep having to give back to God. They are no good to me, and only God knows just what to do with them, as I surely do not. Holding on to worries only makes the head hurt, the heart race, and the legs become weak. I often wonder what God does with all our anxieties. Where do they go? Perhaps into the pits of hell. I do not know. I only know when peace settles in, and for that, my heart is overwhelmingly grateful, and my momma's voice will always remain number one.

Prayer: Dear Lord, in this world, we have so much to be thankful for. Help me this day to begin a new journey with You, one that is filled with anticipation, joy, wonderment, and gratitude. Thank You for the blessings and opportunities You afford me. I am most grateful for Your wonderful gift of salvation through Your Son, Jesus Christ. Amen.

Reflective scripture: "You are my God, and I give thanks to You; You are my God, I exalt You. Give thanks to the Lord, for He is good; For His mercy is everlasting" (Psalm 118:28–29 NASB).

Leaving Your Mark

There he stood in all his glowing glory for my eyes only. What in the world would possess a grown man to wear glow-in-the-dark chartreuse shorts? Well, a runner who is running in the early morning light was the answer! He sure did stand out and made me chuckle a bit, looking so serious and all leaning against the stop sign as he awaited crossing the road.

I was making my way down the winding road at 6:00 a.m. on my way to an early exercise class and having a conversation with God about people leaving their mark on this world. I was wondering what my own responsibility might be and was trying to discern if leaving one's mark is even necessary. I mean, Jesus doesn't love us based on our doings and performances, but He does expect us to use our gifts for Him, so in my head, I was trying to discern what was right for me at this time in my life. Perhaps you, too, are trying to figure this out, or maybe you have found the right balance. If so, that is wonderful, so keep on shining!

Anyway, I was jarred away from my head conversation when I noticed the man in the glow-in-the-dark shorts standing on the side of the road. *Now, there is someone who is leaving his mark*, I thought, and he doesn't even know it. A big revelation followed. Wow, perhaps it really isn't necessary if we *know* we are leaving a mark. Not knowing we are leaving a mark or impression makes our "unintentional acts" all that more sincere.

What God wanted to reveal to me that morning was just like I noticed the man in the early morning, God sees us. Yes, He does. *He sees you!* He knows when our intentions are of Him receiving the glory and not ourselves. The chartreuse-green shorts stood out. They reflected light in order to protect the runner. We, too, are called in this life to "glow in the dark" for Christ. Our intentions should not be to stand out but to glorify God in our works. Thanks be to God for the man leaning against the stop-sign post, unaware of his message to me…and you.

Prayer: Thank You, God, for the various and many surprising ways in which You speak. Help me this day to shine my light, keep my heart pure for You, and to always point any areas of glorification back to You. Amen.

Reflective scripture: "As in water, face reflects face, so a man's heart reveals the man" (Proverbs 27:19 NKJV).

Good Gifts

Did you ever receive a gift that was the worst gift ever? I mean, you have no clue what to do with it. You never asked for it. It's not very attractive, not functional, and of no value to your life whatsoever. The Bible says that "every good gift and every perfect gift is from above, and cometh down from the Father of lights" (James 1:17a KVV).

It was 2:36 a.m., and my brain did not want to sleep. Sometimes when I get this way, I recite in my head the alphabet with scripture. For instance, A: "And this shall be a sign unto you: Ye shall find the babe wrapped in swaddling clothes, lying in a manager" (Luke 2:12 KJV). B: "Be ye kind one to another, tenderhearted, forgiving one another" (Ephesians 4:32a KJV). C: "Casting all your cares upon Him; for He cares for you" (1 Peter 5:7 KJV). You get the point. So when I made it to E, "Every good and perfect gift is from above," it got my spirit stirred.

Is every gift from God good? How about when you get fired from a job, your spouse leaves you, your child is taken away from you too soon, you are diagnosed with an illness that perhaps will be a long battle? Is it good?

I feel certain that James was letting us know in the scripture that when good comes our way, then that gift of good is from God and that we should be quick to thank Him for the goodness and blessings that come our way. But back to my original question: can perceivably "bad gifts" be good?

I am sure, like myself, you have heard people refer to bad times as blessings in disguise. I have had my own experiences with this.

Could not see the good in the situation at the time but was able to reflect back and see God's hand at work. But did that make the bad situation suddenly a good gift? When we do not understand God's way, we can often trust. Sometimes our human desires get in the way of God. We are wise to step aside and let Him be God in our circumstances. It is hard to do at times, I know. Find a friend to confide in or a godly mentor if your situation becomes too painful. Do not attempt to walk the journey alone.

Often, these unperceived gifts become stepping stones to other pathways, adventures, and journeys with God that can be rewarding, and no one can put a price tag on the value of walking with God hand in hand. You may not like the circumstance you have been placed in, and yes, it may and will be hard, but God encourages us to unwrap His mercies and grace and move forward in the journey. Remember that prayer changes things. It is true for all of us. Cling to that. Trust that. Go with that!

Prayer: Thank You, God, for Your many gifts, gifts that often go unwrapped and unnoticed, gifts that just sit and go unused. Thank You that Your mercy and grace come in many forms. Help me to walk with You hand in hand even when I do not understand where You are leading. Amen.

Reflective scriptures:

> **Every good and perfect gift is from above, coming down from the Father of the heavenly light, who does not change like shifting shadows. (James 1:17 NIV)**

> **If you then, being evil, know how to give good gifts to your children, how much more will you Father who is in heaven give good things to those who ask Him! (Matthew 7:11 NKJV)**

Contagious Joy

Encounters, God moments—we all have them, and I pray God keeps giving them to me. God moments can happen every day if we are paying attention. I had one in Florida as my husband and I were leaving the grocery store. One of the employees grabbed my cart and said he was going to push it to my car and unload the large packages of water and various other food we had purchased. My husband and I laughed and thought it was a joke because the man was being so darn friendly and nice. We must have looked a bit bewildered, and the man reassured us he wanted to do this service. We had been to this grocery store several times in the past, and never before had anyone ever offered to push our cart and unload our groceries. Perhaps we looked a bit desperate!

We learned that the gentleman was from Haiti, and he said he was happy to be working. I could not get over his genuine display of joy. It was contagious. He would not accept a tip, which made him even more genuine. He opened my car door and waved goodbye as we drove off. The gentleman treated us like guests in his home, giving us a hearty send-off.

I had tears in my eyes because of his kindness. You see, we had been traveling all day. I was tired and was apprehensive about traveling and leaving home. That encounter really lifted my spirits, leaving me feeling refreshed. The kind man in the green long-sleeved shirt from Haiti, with a smile as broad as anything I have even seen, made my day at the close of the evening. His joy was contagious. That is what I want to have, contagious joy!

Where can you spread joy in the lives of others today? A small act of kindness can truly go a long way to refreshing the spirit of someone in need.

Prayer: Lord, help me to remain in the spirit of joy. Help me to spread joy and love of You to others even when I am weary. May joy in You be an everyday experience. Amen.

Reflective scripture: "Be glad in the Lord, and rejoice, ye righteous: and shot for joy, all ye that are upright in heart" (Psalm 32:11 KJV).

Just a Little Talk with Jesus

It was an early day in spring. The sky was filled with a painting of colors. The tulip trees, the forsythia, the crepe myrtles, the pear trees—it was just a joy to drive down the road. The previous day, I had observed a couple sitting on their front porch as I drove by. They seemed deep in conversation, and it brought a tear to my eye as I thought of the many times over the years I had observed my own momma and stepdad doing the same thing. There is nothing like a good conversation with a loved one shared with a glass of cold, sweet tea or a satisfying cup of coffee.

On this particular spring day, I bypassed the same house, and the couple was not on the porch. The chairs were empty but facing each other. This simple placement of the chairs said to me that the couple would be returning and looked forward to what the other had to say. I smiled as I thought about Jesus waiting for us each day to come, sit, turn our chairs toward Him, and unload that which concerns our hearts.

Jesus has much to say to us when we take the time to sit in His presence. His chair is never empty, and He always saves a seat for us. He is ever present to be listening to all that we need to say.

Life can be difficult at times, and we need each other to get through the journey. We are each carrying loads that get far too heavy sometimes, and Jesus never meant for us to bear anything alone. His grace is always available, and we can stay fulfilled if we take the time to slow down.

An old song comes to mind: "Just a Little Talk with Jesus."[1] One verse says,

> I may have doubts and fears, my eyes be filled with tears, but Jesus is a friend who watches day and night. I go to Him in prayer, He hears my every care, and Just a Little Talk with Jesus makes it right.

I grew up singing and listening to that song, and the message is so simple. Just a little talk with Jesus sure does make everything right. Now let us go…and sit a spell with Him.

Prayer: Thank You, heavenly Father, that You are always available to talk with us. Thank You for the times in which You have slowed us down long enough to hear the sweet, gentle whisper of Your voice. May it never, ever be out crowded by life. Amen.

Reflective scripture:

> **The gatekeeper opens the gate for him, and the sheep recognize his voice and come to him. He calls his own sheep by name and leads them out. After he has gathered his own flock, he walks ahead of them, and they follow him because they know his voice. They won't follow a stranger; they will run from him because they don't know his voice. (John 10:3–5 NLT)**

---

[1] Cleavant Derricks, *Church Hymnal* (Cleveland, Tennessee: Stamps-Baxter Music Co., 1937), 92.

From the Window

He wasn't old, nor was he young, for I never saw him in terms of age. He was just a man who sat by his window from inside his home and waved to me every afternoon or early evening on most occasions as I walked my dog. We had exchanged very few words over the years, being distant neighbors, and I rarely saw him outside his house, but we had some sort of relationship that was familiar and comforting from the window.

From outside, I could see that his window seat was perhaps a comfy recliner, and I would often see the glow of the TV from the corner of his room at night. His faithful labradoodle was sure to be either by his side with his face comfortably resting on the windowsill or one window up from his master, peeking to see the outside world.

The view of Fred and his dog always lifted my spirits—I outside walking my dog, he inside with his fur baby. We would smile and wave heartily to each other. But weeks would go by, and Fred was no longer by the window.

I began to suspect something was wrong. Then just as quickly as he disappeared, he reappeared one evening by his window. His smile warm, his wave hearty, and his head a bit bald. I suspected the dreaded C word. I debated going to his door, saying hello in person, but there was something private about our relationship. A distant respect that was okay among neighbors.

Weeks later, the ambulance came, the fire trucks roared, and the sheriff showed up. Fred was not only gone from the window but from life.

I miss him. I shed a tear this day in the rain as I walked by his house. I gaze at the window and am sorry that I never let him know how much his wave and appearance by the window uplifted me. But I think he knew. Somehow, a face-to-face meeting would have ruined the unspoken.

We don't always have to have a face-to-face encounter for something or someone to impact us. Sometimes the unspoken action is enough. Thank you, Fred, from the window. I shall miss you. I pray you have a comfortable viewing seat from heaven. Your wave was enough to encourage me to keep on walking the journey. After all, life is a true gift.

Prayer: Thank You, God, for the people who encourage us along life's journey. Thank You for the precious gift of life, and may we never waste a second. Help me this day to be an encourager to another even if the action is only a gentle wave. Amen.

Reflective scriptures:

> **We are here only for a moment, visitors, and strangers in the land as our ancestors were before us. Our days on earth are like a passing shadow, gone so soon without a trace. (1 Chronicles 29:15 NLT)**

> **For God so loved the world, that he gave his only begotten Son, that whosoever believeth in him should not perish, but have everlasting life. (John 3:16 KJV)**

A God-Appointed Time

Settle in. This is a long one, but I pray it is hopefully worth your time! As I was reading a devotion one afternoon, the thought came to my spirit to pray for a 1959 penny, which just happens to be my birth year. This penny would serve as a way of encouragement to me that God was going to help me overcome a particular thing in my life that was causing me to experience anxiety.

During this time, I was also involved in a Bible study on the book of Esther. Through the study, I was reminded of the many times in my life that God had seen me through and all the various ways He used to encourage me. In difficult times, we have to remember what God has done for us personally, and we need to recount those stories repeatedly in our minds and hearts. I was encouraged by my remembrances and kept praying about my situation.

During this time, which was in January, my uncle in North Carolina passed away, and I needed to board a plane for his funeral. The interesting thing is I experienced a panic attack one time many years ago while flying, so it was difficult for me to fly at times. I have never experienced a panic attack on a plane since that one time, but I never forgot it. Now the other interesting thing is I had been praying to be released from anxiety while on an airplane so I could enjoy my travels more. Bravely, I made the uneventful flight to Charlotte, and after getting my rental car, I stopped at a drugstore to purchase some water and gum and resume my travels by car to my family's home two hours away.

Two days later, I was leaving North Carolina to return to Salisbury by plane. I treated my sister to breakfast before leaving. As

I was getting ready to pay for our purchase, I got out my wallet, and it had become my habit to check the dates on pennies before handing them over. To my surprise, when I looked through my change, there was a 1959 penny! I was utterly speechless, for you see, that day in that restaurant with that 1959 penny lying in my hand was my birthday, and the penny was my birth year, and it was answered prayer!

The most incredible thing is, I had only made one purchase that whole weekend, and it was the bottle of water and gum at the drugstore after getting off that plane. I purposely cleaned out my wallet of any loose change before leaving on my trip. My heart leapt with joy, and I had my sister check the date just to make sure I was not seeing things. What a gift!

God will do incredible things for us to encourage us and remind us that *He knows our name!* It was a formidable experience for me regarding my faith, and just the sheer excitement that God surprised me on my birthday was amazing! I started thinking about all the events that had to happen in order for the '59 penny to land in my hand on exactly my birthday. I had to face my fears and get on that airplane. I had to trust God with my anxiety and relax in Him. God put the desire for water and gum in my mind, knowing he had a 1959 penny just waiting for me at that particular drugstore.

To think about the cashier putting the penny into my hand without my even stopping to look due to being in a hurry to get to my family just causes my heart to feel so loved by God. Think about how many hands that little penny had to pass through in order to get to my hand. The sheer fact that I had not purchased anything in those two days was also amazing. I had no need to go into my wallet until the morning of my birthday.

When I stop and think about the perfect timing of it all, it just overwhelms my spirit! That 1959 penny is locked in my safe. It is the most cherished gift I own. I know it came directly from the hand of God. It is priceless and far outweighs any earthly possession I own.

I know that God will reward our obedience and will move mountains for all believers. He desires nothing more than to speak to us through circumstances and to show us how much He loves us. He truly delights in surprising us!

This story is reserved not just for me. God wants to speak to you through circumstances as well. His love and experiences are reserved for *all* believers. Cherish those God experiences that He has given you. He does it because He loves you. There are no coincidences in this life, just God-appointed times.

Prayer: Almighty God, thank You for the ways You show Your love to me. Thank You for caring about every minute detail of my life. Thank You for surprises, delights, and the unending ways You encourage. Amen.

Reflective scripture: "For Jehovah God is our Light and our Protector. He gives us grace and glory. No good thing will he withhold from those who walk along his paths" (Psalm 84:11 TLB).

Extra reflection: If you have a hard time believing that God is a God of happy surprises, then I encourage you to begin a journal. Title your page "God Surprises" and jot down two or three desires of your heart and begin to pray about them. See what happens and expect God to hear you. Journal your thoughts about your journey regarding "God Surprises."

God Is Love

"Alexa, tell me a Bible verse!" I said one bright spring morning. "God loves you!" she replied.

I don't have a habit of interacting with artificial intelligence, but my curiosity was such that I was so inclined to ask the all-knowing square box to tell me a Bible verse just to see if she was programed to do so. Turns out she is!

Alexa was not the first to tell me that God loves me but certainly the first mechanical device to do so. After she enthusiastically quoted her scripture, it got me to thinking about when I first knew that God loved me. I had grown up having "God loves you" instilled in me, but when did I first truly know it in my heart? Turns out, it has taken a while.

I grew up believing that God was hard and someone to fear. I had a hard time feeling connected to Him because of my own difficulties with other men in my life (I learned this much later in life). But I began to reflect and found myself grateful for all the people who had helped me along in my spiritual journey. Learning about God's love is an eternal lesson as long as we are on this earth. We see it, feel it, learn it, grow from it, and experience it in various ways.

I was just having fun with Alexa that day, just testing the square box's intelligence. She is of great use sometimes when I might need a recipe or a quick answer to something regarding spelling or definition, but her true value hinged on the question, does "she" know about Jesus? Turns out "she" does. I am unsure from where she quoted her scripture exactly, but her message was clear: God loves!

How about you? Do you truly know about Jesus and His love for you? Do you have people close to you who you can talk with and experience spiritual growth? Do you have resources into which you are not tapping? These are all things for us to ponder as we journey through life. We all need to be plugged in to various ways of learning more about God's love so that we can share it and show it to others.

Prayer: Holy Father, help me to grow, learn, study, and commit to memory Your written words and embed them in my heart so that I can recall it at any time. Give me opportunities to share Your love with others. Thank You, God, for loving me. Amen.

Reflective scripture: "And this hope will not lead to disappointment. For we know how dearly God loves us, because he has given us the Holy Spirit to fill our hearts with his love" (Romans 5:5 NLT).

Show, Don't Tell

"I don't want to talk about religion or God," he said.

My heart sank. *How can I have a conversation with someone and not talk about God?* I thought.

Work on the friendship first, God said to my spirit. *Show him Christ through your actions, words, and deeds. Don't just tell. Show.*

My friend doesn't believe in God and doesn't want a relationship with Him. It hurt my heart, but I was determined to hang in there, knowing that God had a purpose for bringing him into my and my husband's life. I remember the day when God told me to say hello and to strike up a conversation with the older man. "I don't like him, Lord. I don't know him, but I have seen how he interacts with others, and I will not speak to Him," I stubbornly declared.

Yes, speak to him, said God in my heart.

Reluctantly, I did as God instructed, and now a year later, my husband and I lunch with him frequently. He took us to his home to meet his dog, cooked dinner for us, and he spent Thanksgiving with my family and held hands with us around the table as we prayed. He gave a resounding *amen* at the end of the prayer. I said, "I knew in my heart you believed."

He said with a twinkle in his eye, "I believe. I just don't talk about it."

Belief, for some, runs deeper than for others, but the depth of belief doesn't matter as much as the fact that we are stepping, growing, and striving to going deeper with God. We are all on different spiritual journeys, I believe. No one is any higher than another. Sure, some people know and have Bible knowledge more than others, but what matters most is that we are at least striving to know Jesus better and that we are walking hand in hand with Him.

Only God knows the privacy of a person's heart, and some people are private about their faith and aren't as quick to share their beliefs with others. My friend has tested my patience over the years, and at one point offended me so deeply, I had to back off speaking with him. But I believe I had something to learn from Him. I saw a bitter man soften up a bit by our reaching out, having lunch, and sharing a meal. His testing of my patience reminded me that God surely becomes impatient with me at times too, but He keeps loving me, walking with me, and allowing me to experience His goodness.

Don't be afraid to reach out to others when the Holy Spirit prompts you to do so. Sometimes our actions speak louder than our words for sure.

Prayer: Show me this day, dear God, someone who needs Your actions of love. May I be quick to be obedient to You, knowing that some encounters are divine appointments. Amen.

Reflective scripture: "The Lord is not slow about His promise, as some count slowness, but is patient toward you, not willing for any to perish but for all to come to repentance" (2 Peter 3:9 NASB).

I'll Be There!

"I be there to help ye if you need me to. I might fall over trying to help, but I sure will be there!" said the man from his hospital bed. I couldn't help but overhear his conversation because of his loud, jovial voice and also because my family member's bed was right next to his in the same hospital room. I do not know to whom the man was speaking with on the other end of the phone, but I gathered it to be a very close friend.

You see, before his phone call, the man had just walked past me on the way to the restroom. He remarked that he was getting older and slower as he shuffled along with his walker. I watched as he became a bit weary due to difficulty breathing, but he persevered.

I was touched that this man, who was struggling so much, had offered to "show up" for somebody else. Show up—sometimes that is all we have to do for others. Be there. Be present. Be a cheerleader. Be an encourager. Be a helper. Or sometimes, just be…with whomever might need us.

The gentleman was sincere in his willingness to help his friend, I just knew. It was his attitude that impressed me the most. Here he was, lying in a hospital bed, and yet he found joy in the moment by his offer to help someone else in need. He laughed at the hospital TV shows, ate crackers that I shared with him, and joked about someone else winning four million dollars. He laughed, he shared, he was present, and he was a bright light.

So that leaves me with this thought: where shall you and I "show up" today? "I'll be there to help ye if you need me to" could easily become a worldwide mantra. If we market it and make a million, I vote we give it to the man in the hospital room. Let's go and put it on a T-shirt!

Prayer: Show me places where I can show up today, dear God. Amen

Reflective scripture:

> **Praise be to the God and Father of our Lord Jesus Christ, the Father of compassion and the God of all comfort, who comforts us in all our troubles, so that we can comfort those in any trouble with the comfort we ourselves receive from God. For just as we share abundantly in the sufferings of Christ, so also our comfort abounds through Christ. (2 Corinthians 1:3–5)**

Wilted Flower

Do you ever feel like a wilted flower in need of refreshing water and nutrients that provide the energy to carry on? Life can get pretty demanding sometimes, leaving us feeling depleted in various ways. We may question where God is in the midst of all our feelings of depletion, but rest assured He is there.

My eye caught the tiny verbena flower that I had plucked from my planter just the day before as I was cleaning out flowerpots, preparing for the cold weather ahead. Most of the flowers were spent, but one tiny flower held on. Carefully, I put the delicate stem in a favorite small vase and placed it on my windowsill, admiring the colors of red and yellow, which lifted my spirits. The next day, the plant was taking on a wilted look because it had been cut from its main stem of nourishment.

Aren't we like that sometimes? When we get disconnected from God and try to handle things in our own strength, we become depleted and wilted. I was feeling like that this particular day because of the demands of caregiving. Caregiving is hard work and at times frustrating. When you feel you are doing all you can to make someone better and it just isn't happening—wilted, disconnected, depleted. But you know, God can help us to carry on. All it takes is for us to cry out to Him, and strength is restored somehow.

It is also during times like this you can feel the prayers of others being lifted up for you. Prayers help restore our strength and make us feel refreshed. Life gets hard, but the prayers of the people still carry on.

One of the best things we can do for ourselves when we are depleted is to pray for others. Somehow, our cries to God take our focus off of ourselves, and in turn, I believe God places our concerns on the hearts of others so that we are prayed for as well. If you feel wilted and depleted, do not be discouraged. Refreshment is on the way, and it is usually just a prayer away.

Prayer: Thank You, God, for being my source of nourishment at all times during all things. Help me to be mindful of the various needs of others and to be diligent in praying for those You place on my heart this day.

Reflective scripture: "And Jesus said to them, 'I am the bread of life. He who comes to Me shall never hunger, and he who believes in Me shall never thirst'" (John 6:35 NKJV).

Seasons

*S*wish, *swish, crunch, crunch. Swish, swish, crunch, crunch.* I see my shadow as the sun warms my backside. A squirrel munches on a pine cone and quickly scurries up a tree. *Snap, snap* as the nuts crunch under my feel. It is raining red and yellow twirls of color. Kids laugh as they jump and run in a twirl of dead, dry debris. Orange and yellow balls adorn every doorstep, and tiny buttons of white, yellow, and burgundy grace the flowerpots to replace the leggy annuals.

Can you guess the season I am describing? Perhaps like me, it is your favorite season too. How would you describe your season? We hear a lot right now about the seasons of our lives. It has nothing to do with the four seasons but more to do with stages of life. We bury our parents, we take care of sick children, we pray, we travel, we laugh, we cry, we give, and we take. We grow older and hopefully wiser, face health challenges, and at the same time, we manage to share our God-given gifts and struggles with others. Seasons come and go. Life happens, we overcome, and we renew.

How would you describe the season of life you are currently facing right now? Can you find God there with you? God is constantly aware of your whereabouts. If you are gliding through, crying through, rejoicing through, trusting through, or questioning through the season of your life, do not go through it without Christ. Rain will come, snow will blow, flowers will come, and leaves will fall, but through it all, our hope rests in Christ. Grab His hand as He gently leads you through the changes, doing your best to trust that it will all be okay whatever the season of your life may bring. Through it all, God remains unchanging.

Prayer: Thank You, dear God, for the many seasons of life that You have brought me through and will continue to. Thank You for the changes in my life that have helped me grow and mature in You. Thank You for challenging times when I have no one to depend upon but You. Thank You for the gentle way You guide me and the grace You bestow. Amen.

Reflective scripture:

> Daniel answered and said: "Blessed be the name of God forever and ever, for wisdom and might are His. And he changes the times and the seasons; He removes kings and raises up kings; He gives wisdom to the wise and knowledge to those who have understanding. He reveals deep and secret things; He knows what is in the darkness, and light dwells with Him. (Daniel 2:20–22 NKJV)

The I AM of Our Life

Awake, can't sleep. In my mind, I ask, *Who are You, God?*
As I reflect on the day, in my spirit, God replied, *I am the answer to all your prayers. I am healing. I am the silence after the rain. I am restoration. I am comfort. I am peace. I am the laughter after the pain. I am the answers to your heart's desires. I am all that one will ever need. I am rest. I am King. I am joy. I am the answer. I am the voice of everything because I AM!*

When we allow God to fill in the blanks of our life, only then can we find true rest. Enough said.

Prayer: God, we as humans cannot fully grasp Your mightiness. We are grateful that You are the Master over all that life might throw our way. Thank You for being the I am of my life. Amen.

Reflective scripture: "When Jesus spoke again to the people, he said, 'I am the light of the world. Whoever follows me will never walk in darkness but will have the light of life'" (John 8:12 NIV).

For further reflection, look up the following scriptures regarding I am. Which one speaks to you at this particular point in your life? John 6:35, John 10:9, John 10:11, John 11:25–26, John 14:6, John 15:5

The Unwavering Hand of God

I magine, if you will, yourself all alone standing on top of a large beach ball and attempting to balance yourself. It can get pretty rocky when we go at life alone. Now imagine yourself on that same ball and the word *God* imprinted in big bold letters on the bottom of the ball. Continue to balance and now grab ahold of an imaginary bar over your head in which the word *steadfast* is written across it. Having the bar overhead tends to help one feel secure and better balanced. It is the same for life. God and steadfastness go together.

I needed the word *steadfast* in my life one day. My little brother reached out to me in regard to an illness my husband was battling. As his caregiver, I was a bit weary. My brother's encouragement with the words to "hold steadfast" was encouraging.

Later that night, the image of balancing a rocking ball and holding on to the bar of steadfastness came to me. Life is really like that, isn't it? We all have things we have to face and juggle, and we, at times, might feel as if we are on a balancing ball. But we can maintain and persevere if we are holding steadfast to God. He is truly our sustainer and supporter in life. He holds on to us with a steadfastness that will never fail no matter how difficult things may seem. What a comfort that is. Now hold on, for God will not let you fall!

Prayer: Lord, when we don't know what to do, thank You that Your resources never run out. Thank You that Your love, Your care, and Your encouragement are steadfast, and Your unwavering hand is always upon me. Amen.

Reflective scripture: "The steadfast love of the Lord never ceases; his mercies never come to an end; they are new every morning; great is your faithfulness."

A New Season

I looked from my window, noticing that the leaves on the plant had started to turn brown. I mentally beat myself up for another job that had not been accomplished. I would have, in the past, moved the plant indoors and nursed it through the winter, but this season, I did not have the time or the energy. "Let it go," I quietly told myself.

Sometimes, seasons of our lives will not permit us to accomplish all that we have in the past. And sometimes, what we had deemed important in the past is no longer of importance today. Wonder why that happens? I do not really have the answer, only perhaps to say that we run out of energy, or life has become busier in other ways, and we have to prioritize areas of our lives more carefully as we age. Nothing wrong with that. It just is.

I feel for the little plant dying in the winter chill, but starting over next spring or summer will be refreshing too. Truth be known, the plant didn't seem to be doing very well even before winter set in. Do you ever feel like that too, that you aren't doing very well? If we are honest, we all have moments like that. It is okay. You will be okay. God will nourish you, refresh you, and bring you back to life. It might take rest, getting more off your plate, and dying to things that are no longer important. Whatever it is that God is telling you to let go of, just do it. A new season is coming, so rest up and get excited!

Prayer: Lord, show me things that need to be pruned and deleted from my life. Continue to guide me toward things that are important to You and to let go of things that no longer need to be part of my life. Amen.

Reflective scripture: "Behold, I am going to do something new; Now it will spring up; Will you not be aware of it? I will even make a roadway in the wilderness, rivers in the desert" (Isaiah 43:19 NASB).

Full Circle

The little bug had me fascinated as I watched his little black and orange body race around the white knob of my mailbox flap. Around and around, he went in a continuous circle of nowhere. I watched in disbelief that he kept doing the same thing over and over. It made me anxious to watch him continuously race in a zone of going nowhere. Relief for him came when I stuck a pine needle in his pathway, and he climbed aboard, and I gently put him on the pathway of a more productive trail.

Then it hit me: the answer I had been waiting for as to whether to end a ministry I had started six years ago. I had begun to feel that the ministry had come full circle. I was tormented with thoughts that I would be disappointing God or others if the ministry ended. God had ordained it, so was He really telling me to end it? Should I, or should I not?

It took me seeing a little bug racing in a continuous circle for me to recognize myself. I had been praying and searching and talking to friends and committee members and family members as to what to do when God had already told me in my heart what to do: "You've come full circle."

Sometimes it is hard to walk away from the familiar, but as I walked away from my mailbox after putting the little bug on a new pathway, I knew in my spirit that God would be doing the same for me. I wasn't giving up a ministry. I was just sitting my feet on new ground. I knew what I had to do.

Life gets crazy sometimes, and so many things can pull us in so many directions. Around and around we go. When you are faced with a major decision, hold tight to God. He will direct and lead you and show you the pathway you are to travel. He never intends for us to go round and round in circles. Pause and ask God to help you find your way. Watch out for interruptions as they can be blessings in disguise providing just the relief you need.

Prayer: Thank You, God, for interruptions in my life as they can sometimes serve to show us another way. Thank You that with You, there are endings and new beginnings. Amen.

Reflective scripture: "Many plans are in a person's heart, But the advice of the Lord will stand" (Proverbs 19:21 NASB).

God's Night Light

(A reflection at the close of the day)

I see You, Lord. In so many ways, I see You. Thank You for seeing me.

I bowed on my knees by my bedside at the close of the day. The moon was peeking in at me through the slats of the shutters. I see You, Lord. The moon's soft glow was so beautiful, showing off its hues of nighttime colors. Sometimes God allows us a front-row seat. I think I'll sleep with the shutters open tonight, just me, the moon, and God. Thank You, God, for seeing me.

Where did God show up for you today? Give Him thanks and praise!

Prayer: Thank You, God, for showing up every day in my life. Help me to always see You and to reflect on You at the close of the day. Amen.

Reflective scripture:

> **When I consider Your heavens, the work of Your fingers, The moon, and the stars, which You have ordained, what is man that you are mindful of him, And the son of man that You visit him? For You have made him a little lower than the angels, and you have crowned him with glory and honor. (Psalm 8:3–5 NKJV)**

Nestled in a Manger

The minister's stole flowed freely as he turned to give the blessing. It was only then that I noticed a needlepoint stitching of baby Jesus nestled in His manger, snuggled with a halo overhead.

What a great feeling that must have been to be safe and secure in a manager in an unpredictable world, no different than our world today. Just as Baby Jesus did not know at the time of His birth what His destiny would hold, we, too, have to trust that God will reveal our destiny step-by-step in life. It really is a faith thing. Just one day at a time and one moment are all that really is given.

No need to fear. We can feel fear, but just as Jesus did, we persevere even when we know not what lies ahead. Life will present challenging times, and we might not always feel the safety of being wrapped in a blanket and safe in a manager, but God holds us securely and cradles us even when we feel uncertain and afraid.

There are various ways that God snuggles us in a manager. He embraces us through other people when we are hurting, He places the right words in front of us at just the right time to provide direction (the Bible), He loves us unconditionally, and He forgives us when we fall out of the cradle and land in places that we cannot figure out how we even got there. Thank goodness that God's mercy allows us to start over in life.

The image on the minister's vestment will remain a powerful image throughout this Christmas season and even into the New Year, but it doesn't have to be Christmas to see or feel God's embrace and gentle hand as he rocks us through life.

Prayer: Thank You, God, for the truth of Your Son lying in a manager. Thank You for being the true gift to the world. Thank You that Your hand of protection always surrounds me. Amen.

Reflective scripture: "For I am the Lord your God who takes hold of your right hand and says to you, do not fear; I will help you" (Isaiah 41:13 NIV).

A Slap in the Face

One day I passionately told someone that they "wouldn't recognize a blessing even if it slapped them in their face." Not a very nice way to put it, I know, and I am ashamed of that, but I felt passionate that this is sometimes the mindset of individuals and the world, me included.

We get so busy and focused on what we want or think we need that we can't seem to notice anything else. Sometimes God is gently tapping us on the shoulder, saying, "Hey, how about this? Did you notice I did *this* for you? Or how about that prayer I answered for you?"

We get so focused on the goal of getting our needs met that we miss the blessings along the journey. Even interruptions can be a blessing. I am going through a major interruption in my life as I type this. Things are not going as I had planned, and that is my first mistake: what *I* had planned. I think God allows us to make plans, but we must agree with His will for our lives. After all, it is God for whom we are living.

Sometimes interruptions are necessary to help get us back on track. How do you handle interruptions in life? They can sometimes make me irritable, especially when I have goals set and a timeline in mind. But God doesn't work according to our timeline, does He? No, He has His specific plans for each of us and blessings and interruptions and blessings and blessings and blessings! We must follow His agenda, and that includes bowing to His will.

Let us pray that God does not have to metaphorically slap us in the face to make us wake up to His abundance and constant blessings! He is a source of blessings, peace, and joy even when our plans are interrupted or halted.

Thank God for five blessings that you are aware of this moment. See if you can increase the number daily.

Prayer: Your blessings are many, oh God. Thank You for Your presence in my life and even for the interruptions. Forgive me when I become so focused on my own desires that I miss the true blessings right in front of me.

Reflective scriptures:

> **Many are the plans in a person's heart, but it is the Lord's purpose that prevails. (Proverbs 19:21 NIV)**

> **"Bring all the tithes into the storehouse, that there may be food in My house, and try Me now in this," says the Lord of Hosts, "If I will not open for you the windows of heaven and pour out for you such blessings that there will not be room enough to receive it." (Malachi 3:10 NKJV)**

Savor the Savior

It's Christmas Eve, and I don't feel very Christmassy. Not sure why, and perhaps that bothers me the most. Do you ever long for that special feeling as a child when you bounced down the steps at 3:00 a.m. to witness the wonderment of Santa? Not every child has had this experience, but I remember some Christmas pasts that made my little heart sing. I guess as kids, we are all wrapped up in the "What did I get?" mentality. But even as a kid, I remember the warmth that my heart felt and the magic of the season.

Tonight, I took a walk under the cold December sky and looked at all the bright lights among the quiet houses. My day had been spent indoors in my pajamas due to the extremely low temperatures. As I ventured out, my spirit was quiet and wondering if the feeling of Christmas would come this year. *Perhaps it would arrive during the church service later this evening*, I thought.

The indoor heat felt extremely good as I reentered my home graced with my own Christmas decor. I was thankful. I went to the nativity scene that I put up every year and removed Baby Jesus from His manager. "You are focused on the wrong things," I told myself. And I was. I was focused on what wasn't instead of what was. Do you ever find yourself doing the same thing?

I sat down and held the small figurine in my hand, savoring the Savior. The baby's hands were outstretched, as if He wanted someone to pick Him up, just like a tiny infant might do. Even as a child, Christ was ready to receive us. His hands remained outstretched even in death. Sometimes, I find it hard to fathom the sacrifice. For me, for us, for the world—what a gift *He* truly is!

I decided to keep Baby Jesus out of His manager until tomorrow, Christmas morning. There are no wrapped presents under the tree for me this year, something my husband and I agreed upon. We have all we need. I am certain that Jesus is the true gift. We need nothing else. The feelings of Christmas and all its magic tend to disappear when we become adults, but I must say, I am feeling a little excited about placing Baby Jesus in His manger tomorrow morning. I will celebrate His arrival with joy and thanksgiving! It doesn't have to be Christmas to savor the Savior.

Prayer: Holy Father, thank You for the gift of Christmas that we have access to every day of the year. May Your grace sustain us throughout our days, and may we joyfully worship You all the days of our life! Amen.

Reflective scripture: "And this shall be a sign unto you; Ye shall find the babe wrapped in swaddling clothes, lying in a manger" (Luke 2:12 KJV).

It Don't Matter

One of my beautiful nieces has a favorite saying that she coined while living with me and my husband during her time at college. When something of importance or concern was being discussed, she would break the seriousness of the conversation with her spirited words of wisdom: "It don't matter."

At times, I grew frustrated because of her lackadaisical approach to life, but one day I began to think a little deeper about those three words and how they might ring true in some situations. We all know there are very serious matters in this life, and some things are not to be taken lightly, but a lot of times, we do take things too seriously.

I found myself saying these three words periodically when an *issue* would arise, and you know, I found the words to be freeing. It wasn't that I had a nonchalant approach to life, certainly far from the truth, but the three words helped me to put things in perspective. I began to share my niece's coined phrase with friends, and they, too, found themselves saying it at times.

Another coined phrase that you might be familiar with is "God's got this!" For me, that is basically saying, "It don't matter," because when God's got *this*, we have to trust that it is all part of His plan, and that gives us permission to worry less.

Ask yourself, "What is my *this* at this time in my life?" What issue in your life is causing you distress or worry? Where in your life can you apply the phrase, "It don't matter," or "God's got this"? Learn to let go of things. Let God have control. It is far better to let Him work out the unknown than it is for us to get ahead of Him and take the lead.

Perhaps you can create your own phrase that gives your heart freedom and helps to make the load a little lighter. Do not be afraid to ask your heart what it needs. God cares about every matter of the heart. Remember, He's got this, and it don't matter what it is, for God is capable of handling it all. Thanks be to Him!

Prayer: Thank You, God, for simple words that help define who You are. Thank You for caring about every aspect of my life. Thank You for seeing my heart, knowing my desires, and causing all things to work together. I release to You this day all need to control and ask You to be Lord of my life. Amen.

Reflective scripture: "Above all else, guard your heart, for everything you do flows from it" (Proverbs 4:23 NIV).

Only God

Well, here we are. The last devotion. The pressure is on with what to leave you. What do I write as I close out, hopefully leaving you the reader with something to hold on to? The only thing I can say is, "Hold on to the one and only God!" Times will be tough, but they will also be good. Times will be challenging in various ways, but God is with you in the journey. It matters not where you are walking with Him just as long as you are walking…with Him. Remember that His lovingkindness and grace are unending.

Only God can handle our burdens, our worries, our anxieties, our woes. Only God can create beauty out of misery. Only God can help when our human efforts are exhausted. That is why we are wise to turn to Him first. Only God knows the desires of your heart. Only God knows what is truly best for you. Only God can see where you cannot. Only God can provide the means when we see no way out. Only God can rescue the perishing and can make sense out of this seemingly crazy but beautiful world. Only God can help us see the good in all people.

If you haven't claimed Him as Lord and Savior of your life, turn to the one and only God this world has ever known. He is ever ready to embrace you, to love you, to give you your heart's desires. Only God understands you like none other. Only God can do all these things for you—yes, for you.

Never stop being grateful for the people He places in your life and the experiences you have. Share your joys and concerns with others. Trust that God is working and be excited about your journey with Him. Get to know Him better by listening for His voice, studying His Word, and learning His ways. He is forever authoring your story and will do so until eternity. When we meet Him face-to-face, we will know only God, and that will be enough.

Prayer: God, You reign supreme over all. You are the one and only God. Thank You for the stories You write in my life. Thank You for the opportunities You provide to make a difference in this world. Help me to do my best to help others. Help me to rely on You. Help me be all that I can be for You and to let Your light shine. Amen.

Reflective scripture: "Yet for us there is but one God, the Father, from whom all things came and for whom we live; and there is but one Lord, Jesus Christ, through whom all things came and through whom we live" (1 Corinthians 8:6 NIV).

About the Author

Cynthia Holloway resides on the Eastern Shore of Maryland with her hubby and adorable cocker spaniel. She is passionate about deepening her faith and sharing her lessons of learning with others.

Cynthia is a licensed clinical counselor and enjoys hearing the life stories of others and helping them to find God in everyday life events. She credits her grandparents for instilling in her a belief in God that has remained a constant.

Cynthia was a contributing writer for anthology book *Whispers of Grace*, and her first published book was *Fingerprints of God: 62 Day Devotional to Finding God in Ordinary Circumstances*, a 2023 Christian Indie Author's Award Finalist. On a good day, you will find her quietly sitting in her favorite chair, journaling about God and life and the happenings of the moment.